ClearRevise®

AQA GCSE
English Literature

Illustrated revision and practice

Worlds and Lives
Poetry Anthology

Published by
PG Online Limited
The Old Coach House
35 Main Road
Tolpuddle
Dorset
DT2 7EW
United Kingdom

sales@pgonline.co.uk
www.clearrevise.com
www.pgonline.co.uk
2024

PREFACE

Absolute clarity! That's the aim.

This is everything you need to ace the question on *Worlds and Lives* and beam with pride. The content is laid out in a beautifully illustrated format that is clear, approachable and as concise and simple as possible.

The checklist on the contents pages will help you keep track of what you have already worked through and what's left before the big day.

We have included worked exam-style questions with answers for every poem. There is also a set of exam-style questions for you to practise writing answers for. You can check your answers against those given at the end of the book.

LEVELS OF LEARNING

Based on the degree to which you are able to truly understand a new topic, we recommend that you work in stages. Start by reading a short explanation of something, then try to recall what you've just read. This will have limited effect if you stop there but it aids the next stage. Question everything. Write down your own summary and then complete and mark a related exam-style question. Cover up the answers if necessary but learn from them once you've seen them. Lastly, teach someone else. Explain the poem in a way that they can understand. Have a go at the different practice questions – they offer an insight into how and where marks are awarded.

Design and artwork: Jessica Webb / PG Online Ltd

First edition 2024   10 9 8 7 6 5 4 3 2 1
A catalogue entry for this book is available from the British Library
ISBN: 978-1-916518-13-1
Copyright © PG Online 2024
All rights reserved
No part of this publication may be reproduced, stored in a retrieval system, or transmitted in any form or by any means without the prior written permission of the copyright owner.

This product is made of material from well-managed FSC®-certified forests, recycled materials, and other controlled sources.
Printed by Bell & Bain Ltd, Glasgow, UK.

THE SCIENCE OF REVISION

Illustrations and words

Research has shown that revising with words and pictures doubles the quality of responses by students.[1] This is known as 'dual-coding' because it provides two ways of fetching the information from our brain. The improvement in responses is particularly apparent in students when they are asked to apply their knowledge to different problems. Recall, application and judgement are all specifically and carefully assessed in public examination questions.

Retrieval of information

Retrieval practice encourages students to come up with answers to questions.[2] The closer the question is to one you might see in a real examination, the better. Also, the closer the environment in which a student revises is to the 'examination environment', the better. Students who had a test 2–7 days away did 30% better using retrieval practice than students who simply read, or repeatedly reread material. Students who were expected to teach the content to someone else after their revision period did better still.[3] What was found to be most interesting in other studies is that students using retrieval methods and testing for revision were also more resilient to the introduction of stress.[4]

Ebbinghaus' forgetting curve and spaced learning

Ebbinghaus' 140-year-old study examined the rate at which we forget things over time. The findings still hold true. However, the act of forgetting facts and techniques and relearning them is what cements them into the brain.[5] Spacing out revision is more effective than cramming – we know that, but students should also know that the space between revisiting material should vary depending on how far away the examination is. A cyclical approach is required. An examination 12 months away necessitates revisiting covered material about once a month. A test in 30 days should have topics revisited every 3 days – intervals of roughly a tenth of the time available.[6]

Summary

Students: the more tests and past questions you do, in an environment as close to examination conditions as possible, the better you are likely to perform on the day. If you prefer to listen to music while you revise, tunes without lyrics will be far less detrimental to your memory and retention. Silence is most effective.[5] If you choose to study with friends, choose carefully – effort is contagious.[7]

---

1. Mayer, R. E., & Anderson, R. B. (1991). Animations need narrations: An experimental test of dual-coding hypothesis. *Journal of Education Psychology*, (83)4, 484–490.
2. Roediger III, H. L., & Karpicke, J.D. (2006). Test-enhanced learning: Taking memory tests improves long-term retention. *Psychological Science*, 17(3), 249–255.
3. Nestojko, J., Bui, D., Kornell, N. & Bjork, E. (2014). Expecting to teach enhances learning and organisation of knowledge in free recall of text passages. *Memory and Cognition*, 42(7), 1038–1048.
4. Smith, A. M., Floerke, V. A., & Thomas, A. K. (2016) Retrieval practice protects memory against acute stress. *Science*, 354(6315), 1046–1048.
5. Perham, N., & Currie, H. (2014). Does listening to preferred music improve comprehension performance? *Applied Cognitive Psychology*, 28(2), 279–284.
6. Cepeda, N. J., Vul, E., Rohrer, D., Wixted, J. T. & Pashler, H. (2008). Spacing effects in learning a temporal ridgeline of optimal retention. *Psychological Science*, 19(11), 1095–1102.
7. Busch, B. & Watson, E. (2019), *The Science of Learning*, 1st ed. Routledge.

CONTENTS

Assessment objectives vi

Exam technique

The poetry anthology exam question 2
Structuring your answer 3
Planning your answer 4
Writing your answer 5
Technical accuracy 8
Checking your answer 9

Analysis of poems

Lines Written in Early Spring — William Wordsworth 10
   Comparing *Lines Written in Early Spring* 16
England in 1819 — Percy Bysshe Shelley 18
   Comparing *England in 1819* 24
Shall earth no more inspire thee — Emily Brontë 26
   Comparing *Shall earth no more inspire thee* 32
In a London Drawingroom — George Eliot 34
   Comparing *In a London Drawingroom* 40
On an Afternoon Train from Purley to Victoria, 1955 — James Berry 42
   Comparing *On an Afternoon Train from Purley to Victoria, 1955* 48
Name Journeys — Raman Mundair 50
   Comparing *Name Journeys* 56
pot — Shamshad Khan 58
   Comparing *pot* 64
A Wider View — Seni Seneviratne 66
   Comparing *A Wider View* 72
Homing — Liz Berry 74
   Comparing *Homing* 80
A century later — Imtiaz Dharker 82
   Comparing *A century later* 88
The Jewellery Maker — Louisa Adjoa Parker 90
   Comparing *The Jewellery Maker* 96
With Birds You're Never Lonely — Raymond Antrobus 98
   Comparing *With Birds You're Never Lonely* 104

A Portable Paradise — Roger Robinson ...... 106 ☐
   Comparing *A Portable Paradise* ...... 112 ☐
Like an Heiress — Grace Nichols ...... 114 ☐
   Comparing *Like an Heiress* ...... 120 ☐
Thirteen — Caleb Femi ...... 122 ☐
   Comparing *Thirteen* ...... 128 ☐
Overview of themes ...... **130** ☐
Examination practice ...... **131** ☐

Examination practice answers ...... 132 ☐
Levels-based mark schemes for extended response questions ...... 134 ☐
Index ...... 135 ☐
Examination tips ...... **137** ☐

MARK ALLOCATIONS

All the questions in this book require extended responses. These answers should be marked as a whole in accordance with the levels of response guidance on **page 134**. The answers provided are examples only. There are many more points to make than there are marks available, so the answers are not exhaustive.

ASSESSMENT OBJECTIVES

In the exam, your answer will be marked against assessment objectives (AOs). It's important you understand which skills each AO tests.

AO1
- Show the ability to read, understand and respond to texts.
- Answers should maintain a critical style and develop an informed personal response.
- Use examples from the text, including quotes, to support and illustrate points.

AO2
- Analyse the language, form and structure used by a writer to create meanings and effects, using relevant subject terminology where appropriate.

AO3
- Show understanding of the relationships between texts and the contexts in which they were written.

The AOs on this page have been written in simple language. See the AQA website for the official wording.

There are 12 marks available for AO1, 12 marks for AO2 and 6 marks for AO3.

PAPER 2
Modern texts and poetry

Information about Paper 2

Written exam: 2 hours 15 minutes (this includes the questions on modern texts and unseen poetry)

96 marks (30 marks for modern texts plus 4 marks for SPaG, 30 marks for the poetry anthology and 32 marks for unseen poetry)

60% of the qualification grade (20% for modern texts, 20% for the poetry anthology and 20% for unseen poetry)

This guide covers the section on the Worlds and Lives poetry anthology.

Questions

One extended-writing question on a modern text (you will be given a choice of two questions, but you should only answer one), one extended-writing question on the poetry anthology you have studied and two questions on the unseen poems.

THE POETRY ANTHOLOGY EXAM QUESTION

The poetry anthology is tested in Paper 2, along with a question on a modern text you have studied and two questions on unseen poems.

Example question

Here's an example exam-style question for the Worlds and Lives poetry anthology:

> Compare how poets present ideas about identity in *Like an Heiress* and **one** other poem from Worlds and Lives. [30 marks]

How to answer the question

- There will only be one question per anthology: you won't be given a choice of questions.
- You will need to compare the poem specified in the question with one other poem from the Worlds and Lives anthology. It's up to you which poem you choose.
- Don't write about more than one poem in addition to the printed poem. You won't get any extra marks.
- The poem specified in the question will be printed in full. Although you will be given a list of the poems from the anthology, the other poems will not be printed out and you're not allowed to take notes into the exam with you.
- The question will specify a theme. In the example above, the theme is 'identity', but the theme could be anything related to the poems in the cluster: nature, belonging, loneliness, prejudice etc. We've summarised some of the main themes shared across the cluster on **page 130**.
- You will need to write an essay-style response to the question.
- It's not enough to point out techniques used by the poets. You need to comment on their effect on you as the reader, and link them back to the theme.
- This question is worth 30 marks. You should spend about 45 minutes on the question. This includes planning and checking time.

⭐ Your exam paper will also include questions on the **Power and Conflict** and **Love and Relationships** anthologies.

Do not answer questions about poems you have not studied.

STRUCTURING YOUR ANSWER

Most poems can be interpreted in several different ways, and any interpretation is valid as long as you can support your answer with sensible evidence from the poem or the poem's context.

Choosing a poem

In the exam, you will need to decide which poem to compare with the poem given in the question. You should pick a poem which will give you plenty to write about. The poems don't have to share similarities; you can talk about the poems' differences too.

All the poems in the cluster are linked, but some can be compared more effectively than others. When you're revising, you could group poems together by theme, so you can quickly choose a suitable poem in the exam. (Take a look at our handy table on **page 130** to help you.)

We've highlighted some common themes that can be found across the cluster, such as prejudice, oppression, identity and belonging, but these themes aren't exhaustive: there are lots more ways that poems can be thematically linked.

Structuring your answer

There are two main ways you can structure your exam answer.

Option one

You could analyse one aspect of a poem (i.e. a point about language, form, structure or context), and then directly compare how the second poem is similar or different.

Practise answering exam-style questions to see which structure works best for you.

Option two

You could write several paragraphs about the first poem, and then several paragraphs about the second poem.

Whichever structure you choose, make sure your response answers the question.

GCSE English Literature Poetry Anthology | Worlds and Lives

PLANNING YOUR ANSWER

You should spend about five minutes on a plan, but make sure you're happy with your plan before you start writing.

Plan

It's important to jot down a plan before you start writing. This will help make sure that you have enough to write about, and that your answer stays on-track. Think about the comparisons you can make across the poems' content, theme, language, form and structure. You must include details about the poems' context to get full marks.

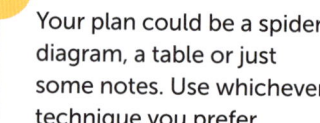

Your plan could be a spider diagram, a table or just some notes. Use whichever technique you prefer.

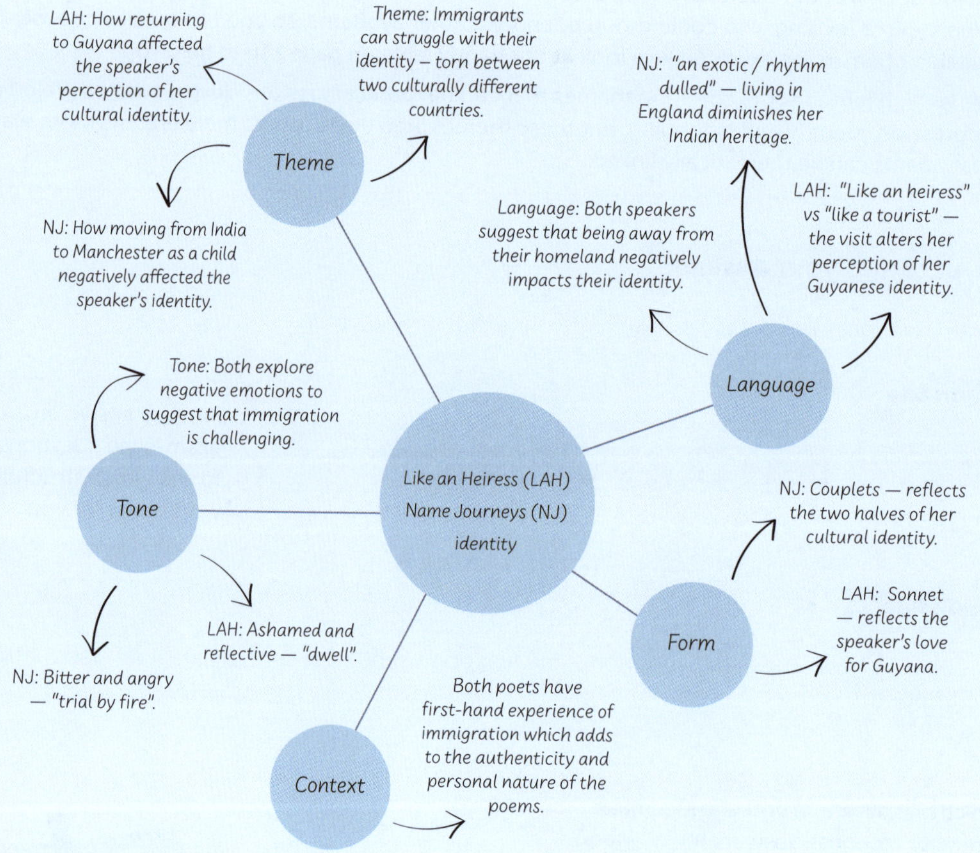

Here's an example plan for the question on **page 2**.

- **LAH:** How returning to Guyana affected the speaker's perception of her cultural identity.
- **Theme:** Immigrants can struggle with their identity — torn between two culturally different countries.
- **NJ:** "an exotic / rhythm dulled" — living in England diminishes her Indian heritage.
- **NJ:** How moving from India to Manchester as a child negatively affected the speaker's identity.
- **Theme**
- **Language:** Both speakers suggest that being away from their homeland negatively impacts their identity.
- **LAH:** "Like an heiress" vs "like a tourist" — the visit alters her perception of her Guyanese identity.
- **Tone:** Both explore negative emotions to suggest that immigration is challenging.
- **Like an Heiress (LAH) / Name Journeys (NJ) identity**
- **Language**
- **NJ:** Couplets — reflects the two halves of her cultural identity.
- **Tone**
- **LAH:** Ashamed and reflective — "dwell".
- **Form**
- **LAH:** Sonnet — reflects the speaker's love for Guyana.
- **NJ:** Bitter and angry — "trial by fire".
- **Context**
- Both poets have first-hand experience of immigration which adds to the authenticity and personal nature of the poems.

⭐ If you're struggling to plan an answer with the poem you've picked, try writing a new plan with a different poem. It's better to spend an extra 5 minutes on another plan than committing to a pair of poems which don't fully answer the question.

WRITING YOUR ANSWER

You should spend about 35 minutes writing your answer.

Introduction

A good introduction should briefly introduce which two poems you are comparing and how they both link to the theme specified in the question. For example:

Example

'Like an Heiress' and 'Name Journeys' explore how immigration can make a person feel confused about their identity. 'Like an Heiress' centres around a speaker who revisits her childhood home of Guyana, whereas 'Name Journeys' focuses on a speaker who was born in India, but immigrated to Manchester as a child. Both speakers suggest that being separated from your home country can lead to feelings of disconnection and can cause individuals to struggle with feelings of belonging.

Main answer

The main part of your answer could compare 3–4 of the following:

- **Form:** What type of poem is it (i.e. sonnet, dramatic monologue)? Does it have a rhyme scheme or is it written in free verse? Whose perspective is the poem told from?
- **Content:** What happens in the poem?
- **Structure:** How many stanzas are there? How are the events ordered and revealed to the reader? Are any lines repeated?
- **Syntax:** How have the lines been constructed? Is there caesura (a deliberate pause in a line), enjambment (when a sentence runs on to the next line), or end-stopping (when a line finishes with the end of a sentence)? Have words been deliberately placed at the start of a line for emphasis?
- **Tone:** What feelings are conveyed by the poem?
- **Language:** What language techniques has the poet used (i.e. alliteration, similes, sensory language)?
- **Theme:** What's the deeper meaning of the poem?
- **Message:** Is the poet trying to tell the reader something?
- **Context:** What was happening at the time the poet was writing which may have influenced the poem?

For every feature you write about, you need to:

- Explain how it answers the question.
- Comment on the effect it has on you as the reader.

You don't need to include examples of all these features. It's far better to write about fewer things in more detail, than lots of things in a limited amount of detail. Remember, a longer answer isn't always a better answer.

You need to comment on context to get marks for AO3 (see **page vi**).

PEEDL

Each paragraph should follow the PEEDL structure: point, evidence, explain, develop and link back to the question.

> You may have been taught a different word such as PETAL, PEEL or PEED, but the idea behind it is exactly the same.

P Point

Choose a feature (look at **page 5** for inspiration) and make a point that relates to the question.

Example

The speaker in 'Like an Heiress' is initially excited to return to Guyana.

E Evidence

Support your point with evidence. This could be a direct quote (which could just be a single word), or an example paraphrased from the poem. Make sure to:

- use **inverted commas** (" ") if you are quoting directly from the poem.
- copy quotes accurately from the poem provided in the exam.
- keep quotes short and relevant.

Example

She describes being "drawn" to the Atlantic Ocean.

E Explain

Explain how the evidence you have selected supports your point. Use linking words to help your answer flow.

This shows...	This reinforces...	This conveys...
This implies...	This hints...	This supports...
This emphasises...	This suggests...	This indicates...

Example

The word "drawn" suggests that the Atlantic Ocean is an almost magnetic force that pulls her towards it, and that the speaker has little control over her overwhelming desire to be on its shores again.

D Develop

Include additional information to develop your point further and comment on the effect that this has on the reader.

Example

The speaker feels a connection to the Atlantic Ocean because it reminds her of her "oceanic small-days". This suggests that she associates the Atlantic Ocean with happy childhood memories.

PEEDL continued

L Link

Link your paragraph back to the question, or link it to your next point.

Example

This reinforces how the speaker's connection to the Atlantic Ocean is part of her life story and it shapes her identity.

Example

Here's an example PEEDL paragraph:

The speakers in 'Like an Heiress' and 'Name Journeys' both struggle with their cultural identities.	This paragraph starts with a **point**
In 'Like an Heiress', the speaker initially compares herself to an "heiress" but she later compares herself to a "tourist".	Then gives an **example** from *Like an Heiress*...
This suggests that she originally thought that returning to Guyana was similar to inheriting something precious, but seeing the rubbish on the beach makes her feel ashamed of her home country so that she no longer wants to associate herself with it.	Followed by an **explanation** of the example.
In 'Name Journeys', the speaker describes how her name becomes "an exotic / rhythm dulled" when it is pronounced by English people.	Then gives an **example** from *Name Journeys*...
This suggests that the speaker feels as though her "exotic" Indian identity has been "dulled" by living in England, and she feels as though she is losing her Indian heritage.	Followed by an **explanation** of the example.
Both speakers suggest that immigration can make it difficult for a person to stay connected to their cultural identity.	This **develops** the point and **links** back to the theme of the question: ideas about identity.

Conclusion

Finish your answer with a brief conclusion. This is the final paragraph where you summarise what you have covered in your answer.

Example

'Like an Heiress' and 'Name Journeys' both suggest that individuals who have immigrated can struggle with their identity and feelings of belonging. Often, immigrants can feel as though they have lost touch with the culture and heritage of their home country while finding it challenging to adopt the culture of their new country. This can make immigrants feel unsure about who are they are and where they belong.

TECHNICAL ACCURACY

To get top marks, you need to make sure your answer uses paragraphs and sophisticated vocabulary.

Paragraphs

Each PEEDL should have its own paragraph. You can signal a new paragraph by starting a new line, and either leaving a gap at the start of the new line or leaving an empty line above it.

Join your paragraphs with linking words to make your answer flow smoothly. For example, if you're adding extra points that agree with or extend your previous point, you could use:

| Firstly / Secondly / Thirdly / Finally… | Furthermore… | Another way that… | In addition… |

If your next point presents an alternative view, you could use:

| However… | Whereas… | Alternatively… | On the other hand… | In contrast… |

Vocabulary

Your answer should be written in Standard English (the form of English that most people agree is correct), and you should avoid using slang or informal language.

- ⊕ Shelley is presented as feeling bitter towards powerful institutions.
- ⊖ Shelley is presented as feeling salty towards powerful institutions.

Use sophisticated, precise language to demonstrate your vocabulary and avoid sounding vague.

- ⊕ The speaker uses sensory language to create a strong sense of place.
- ⊖ The speaker uses lots of good words to describe where the poem is set.

Use technical terms where appropriate to show your knowledge of poetic techniques.

- ⊕ The second stanza uses enjambment which mimics natural speech.
- ⊖ Some lines don't end with full stops which sounds like someone is talking.

CHECKING YOUR ANSWER

You should spend five minutes reading over your answer and correcting any mistakes.

Correcting mistakes

There aren't any marks for SPaG for this question, but you should still make sure your answers are written in full sentences and structured in paragraphs with correct spelling, punctuation and grammar. If your answer is full of mistakes, the examiner might struggle to understand what you have written.

If you spot a mistake, here's how to correct what you've written neatly and carefully:

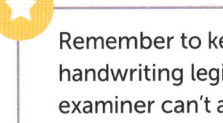

Remember to keep your handwriting legible. The examiner can't award you any marks if they're unable to read what you've written.

Correcting spelling

If you've spelt something incorrectly, carefully cross out the word and rewrite the correction above it.

>   caesura
> The poet uses ~~ceasura~~ to create a pause which focuses the reader's attention.

Adding a missing word

If you've missed a word out, use this symbol ^ where the missing word should go and write the word above it.

>   effect
> The ^ of the alliteration is to mimic how the speaker angrily spits out the words.

Missed paragraph break

If you've forgotten to start a new paragraph, just put // where you want the new paragraph to start.

> ... which encourages the reader to empathise with the speaker. // However, in *Thirteen*, the speaker...

! Note

Learn how to spell tricky technical terms such as 'metaphor', 'simile' and 'onomatopoeia', so you can spell them confidently in the exam.

There aren't any SPaG marks for the anthology questions, but you should still check your answer.

GCSE English Literature Poetry Anthology | Worlds and Lives

LINES WRITTEN IN EARLY SPRING — WILLIAM WORDSWORTH

I heard a thousand blended notes,
While in a grove I sate reclined,
In that sweet mood when pleasant thoughts
Bring sad thoughts to the mind.

5 To her fair works did Nature link
The human soul that through me ran;
And much it grieved my heart to think
What man has made of man.

Through primrose tufts, in that green bower,
10 The periwinkle trailed its wreaths;
And 'tis my faith that every flower
Enjoys the air it breathes.

The birds around me hopped and played,
Their thoughts I cannot measure:—
15 But the least motion which they made
It seemed a thrill of pleasure.

The budding twigs spread out their fan,
To catch the breezy air;
And I must think, do all I can,
20 That there was pleasure there.

If this belief from heaven be sent,
If such be Nature's holy plan,
Have I not reason to lament
What man has made of man?

Annotations:

- The hyperbole of "*a thousand*" emphasises how nature is in harmony.
- Being in nature helps the speaker to relax.
- The half rhyme of "*notes*" and "*thoughts*" hints that not everything is in unity.
- The speaker juxtaposes "*pleasant thoughts*" with "*sad thoughts*", which suggests his despair for humankind is never far from his mind.
- The stressed syllables emphasise the repeated 'ma' sound. This reinforces the idea that humans are responsible for causing one another unhappiness, and have not followed nature's example of living in harmony.
- The speaker uses emotive language throughout to highlight his distress.
- The flowers are personified as being grateful for being alive. This contrasts with humankind's unhappiness.
- The consonance of the repeated 'p' sound matches the bouncy movement of the birds.
- The speaker uses sensory language to describe what he can see and feel. This creates a clear image in the reader's mind.
- This suggests that humans struggle to understand or appreciate nature.
- This line is enjambed, placing "*lament*" at the end of the line to emphasise the speaker's sadness.
- "*holy*" suggests nature is connected to God, and that nature behaves in a pure and righteous way, unlike humans.
- The poem ends with a rhetorical question which encourages the reader to consider their own response.

? **sate** — sat **bower** — a leafy shelter in a wood **lament** — regret sadly

William Wordsworth

William Wordsworth (1770–1850) was an English **Romantic** poet.

The Romantic movement spanned the late 18th century and the first half of the 19th century. Romantic poems were often inspired by nature but also called for societal change.

Lines Written in Early Spring was published in 1798 in a collection called *Lyrical Ballads*.

William Wordsworth

Summary of the poem

The speaker sits in nature, listening to birdsong. He is happy and relaxed, but he begins thinking about more miserable things. He is sad because plants and animals seem to live happily side-by-side, whereas humans treat each other, as well as nature, unkindly.

Context and references

The French Revolution (1789-1799)

By the late 18th century, France was on the verge of bankruptcy, so ordinary French people, faced with economic hardships, rebelled against authority. Revolutionaries arrested the King of France and executed him in 1793. However, following the King's execution, France entered a Reign of Terror between September 1793 and July 1794, where the men who took control of France ordered the arrests of over 300,000 people. Approximately 17,000 people were executed, 10,000 died in prison and thousands more died in massacres. Estimates suggest that over 30,000 people died in this ten-month period, many of whom were ordinary French citizens.

Comment: Reports of the violence in France shocked the British public, and *Lines Written in Early Spring* may be Wordsworth's reaction to humankind's cruelty towards one another.

A scene depicting the Reign of Terror

The Industrial Revolution

The **Industrial Revolution** (c1750-c1840) was the development of factory production in England. It led to an increase in jobs, but factory work was often dangerous and poorly paid. The Industrial Revolution also negatively impacted the environment (see **page 35** for more).

Comment: *Lines Written in Early Spring* could be a criticism of how factory owners treated their workers, and the negative impact that industrialisation had on the environment.

Themes

Oppression

The speaker is saddened by "*What man has made of man*". This hints that humans treat each other unkindly, and could refer to the violence of the French Revolution or the mistreatment of factory workers by their employers.

Spirituality & religion

The speaker believes nature and religion are interconnected (see **page 15**). Nature is "*heaven sent*", suggesting its goodness, which contrasts with humankind's cruelty.

Nature

Positive descriptions of plants and birds present nature as peaceful and unified.

Belonging

The speaker feels disconnected from the world around him.

Form and structure

Ballads

Lines Written in Early Spring was published in a collection of poetry called *Lyrical Ballads*, and it shares some features with a form of poetry called **ballads**.

> **Comment:** It is also an example of a **lyric poem**: a type of poem which expresses personal feelings. The poem is written in the **first person**, which was typical of lyrical poetry.

Most ballads are written in **quatrains** (four-line stanzas), and *Lines Written in Early Spring* is made up of six quatrains. It uses a regular alternating ABAB rhyme scheme, which could reflect the harmony found in nature.

> **Comment:** However, **half rhymes** in the first stanza ("*notes*" and "*thoughts*") disrupt this regular rhyme scheme and hint at the idea of conflict between humans and nature.

Most ballads follow a particular metre: the first and third lines are usually written in **iambic tetrameter** (a rhythm where there are eight syllables on a line, with an unstressed syllable, followed by a stressed syllable), and the second and fourth lines are written in **iambic trimeter** (a rhythm where there are six syllables per line). In *Lines Written in Early Spring*, the third, fourth and fifth stanzas reflect how nature is in unity, so they follow the typical metre found in ballads.

> **Comment:** However, in stanzas 1, 2 and 6, the second line is written in iambic tetrameter, rather than iambic trimeter. These stanzas explore how the speaker is saddened by humankind's behaviour, so this unbalanced rhythm could emphasise how humans are not in unity with each other or the natural world.

⋯ Form and structure continued

The poem's structure emphasises how the speaker is affected by humankind's unpleasantness. The speaker is troubled by "*sad thoughts*" in the first stanza, and he continues to "*lament*" in the final stanza. This **cyclical** structure suggests that the speaker cannot stop feeling sad about the cruel way humans treat each other.

The final two lines introduce a **rhetorical question**: "*Have I not reason to lament / What man has made of man?*". The speaker asks the reader whether his sadness towards humankind is justified, which encourages the reader to consider their own experiences of humanity.

> **Comment:** The rhetorical question is **enjambed**, and the word "*lament*" is placed at the end of the line which emphasises the speaker's sadness.

The rhetorical question also creates an uncertain ending: the speaker doesn't know how to encourage humans to live more harmoniously.

Tone

The poem opens with a peaceful tone. The speaker is in a "*sweet mood*" as he relaxes in nature.

However, the pleasant imagery of nature is repeatedly interrupted by thoughts of humankind's selfishness which creates a tone of despair. The speaker is upset that humans cannot live alongside each other in peace and harmony like plants and animals.

> **Comment:** The speaker doesn't directly acknowledge what has caused him to lose faith in humanity, but at the time the poem was written the French Revolution and the Industrial Revolution were responsible for the suffering of many people (see **page 11**).

Language

Representation of nature

Unified

Nature is presented as being unified: the birds sing "*a thousand blended notes*". The word "*thousand*" is an example of **hyperbole** (exaggeration), which reinforces how the birds work together in harmony.

Comment: The speaker acknowledges that the "*human soul*" was made by "*Nature*". This makes the reader question why humans struggle to live together in harmony.

Soothing

The speaker is at peace when he is surrounded by nature: he thinks "*pleasant thoughts*" and is in a "*sweet mood*".

Comment: The speaker **juxtaposes** his "*pleasant*" thoughts about nature with his "*sad*" thoughts about humanity. This highlights the contrast between the two.

Beautiful

The poem includes lots of pleasant natural images, including "*primrose tufts*", "*green bower*" and "*budding twigs*". This reminds the reader of the beauty and diversity of nature.

Comment: The poem is set in "*Early Spring*". Spring is associated with rebirth and growth after the darkness of winter. The speaker could be hinting that humankind could also emerge from the 'darkness' of the French Revolution and the Industrial Revolution, which gives the poem a sense of hope.

Content

The speaker **personifies** nature as happy and content to enjoy the simple things in life. The flower "*Enjoys*" the air, and the birds "*hopped and played*".

Comment: The **consonance** of the repeated 'p' sound in "*hopped*" and "*played*" reflects the bobbing, playful movement of the birds.

Superior

The speaker comments that nature has "*thoughts I cannot measure*". This suggests that nature is more advanced than humans because it exists in peace and harmony: something that humans are unable to do.

Language continued

Sensory language

The speaker uses **sensory language** to create a clear image of nature in the reader's mind. This sensory language also reinforces how pleasant and relaxing it is being in nature.

 The speaker hears "*a thousand blended notes*".

 He feels "*the breezy air*".

 He sees "*budding twigs*".

Representation of humans

Accountable

The speaker implies that humans are to blame for their problems in the line "*What man has made of man*".

Comment: This line is repeated in the final stanza, reinforcing its significance.

Upsetting

When the speaker thinks about humans, he uses **emotive language** such as "*sad*", "*grieved*" and "*lament*". This suggests he finds human behaviour distressing.

Comment: *Lines Written in Early Spring* is a typical Romantic poem. Romantic poems often drew inspiration from the natural world, but they also included feelings of turmoil and conflict.

Religious language

Comment: Wordsworth was a **Pantheist**: someone who believes that God exists in animals and people. *Lines Written in Early Spring* suggests that being in nature helps the speaker to feel closer to God. However, the speaker also reflects that humans treating nature and other humans with unkindness was like treating God with unkindness.

The speaker uses language associated with religion such as "*soul*", "*faith*" and "*heaven*". Nature is described as having a "*holy plan*", and associating nature with God hints at nature's power. The word "*holy*" also suggests that nature behaves in a righteous way, unlike humans.

COMPARING *LINES WRITTEN IN EARLY SPRING*

Here's how *Lines Written in Early Spring* could be compared to other poems.

 Remember, you can compare *Lines Written in Early Spring* with any poem from the anthology as long as your response is supported with examples. The following examples suggest ways to compare the poems, but they are not complete answers.

Attitudes towards nature

Lines Written in Early Spring presents nature as soothing and beautiful. The speaker is "*sate reclined*" when he is outside in a "*grove*", reinforcing how relaxed he feels in nature. The speaker describes how the birds "*hopped and played*", and the consonance of the 'p' sound mimics their playful, bobbing movements which creates a delightful image for the reader. Being in nature also allows the speaker to think "*pleasant thoughts*", which suggests that he feels calm and happy when he spends time in nature.

However, the speaker in *Like an Heiress* (**page 114**) feels ashamed and guilty when she spends time in nature because it reminds her of humankind's negative impact on the environment. The speaker sees a "*wave of rubbish*" on the beach, and the word "*wave*" suggests that pollution is taking over the ocean. This makes the speaker afraid for the "*quickening years and fate of our planet*", which suggests being in nature makes her feel anxious because she is reminded that time is running out to reverse the damage caused by pollution.

Representation of society

The speaker in *Lines Written in Early Spring* is presented as feeling despondent about the way humans treat one another. Whenever he reflects on society, he uses emotive language, for example: "*sad*", "*grieved*" and "*lament*", which reinforces his miserable mood. The speaker believes that humans are responsible for their own suffering, as he repeats the line "*What man has made of man*". Wordsworth could be alluding to the poor treatment of workers during the Industrial Revolution, as many employees were expected to work long hours in dangerous conditions for little pay. Romantic poets, such as Wordsworth, often wrote poetry which called for societal change.

The speaker in *In a London Drawingroom* (**page 34**) also presents society negatively. The speaker uses the simile "*The world seems one huge prison-house*" to describe London which implies that people are trapped and suffering in the capital. This is reinforced with the phrase "*men are punished at the slightest cost*", which suggests that society is challenging and cruel. Eliot could also be criticising the impact of the Industrial Revolution on London society, and how factory workers in London were forced to suffer terrible conditions.

Compare how poets present ideas about the natural world in *Lines Written in Early Spring* and in **one** other poem from Worlds and Lives. [30 marks]

Your answer may include:

AO1 — show understanding of the poems

- In 'Lines Written in Early Spring', the speaker presents the natural world as harmonious and peaceful. Spending time in nature allows the speaker to relax and feel at ease. Similarly, in 'A Portable Paradise', the speaker presents the natural world as beautiful and peaceful, and he uses thoughts about nature to escape the difficulties in his life.

AO2 — show understanding of the poets' language choices

- Both poems use sensory language to create a vivid sense of the natural world for the reader. In 'Lines Written in Early Spring', the speaker describes what he can hear ("a thousand blended notes"), feel ("the breezy air") and see ("The budding twigs"). In 'A Portable Paradise', the speaker describes what he can smell ("its piney scent"), hear ("its anthem") and see ("white sands"). These descriptions present nature as beautiful.

- Both speakers describe how being in nature makes them feel relaxed and at peace. In 'Lines Written in Early Spring', the speaker "sate reclined" in a "grove". The word "reclined" suggests he was leaning back in a relaxed fashion. In 'A Portable Paradise', the speaker uses thoughts about the natural world to help him "sleep", which suggests that he finds nature relaxing.

- Both speakers imply that life outside of the natural world is challenging. When the speaker in 'Lines Written in Early Spring' thinks about society, he has "sad thoughts". Similarly, the speaker in 'A Portable Paradise', describes the "pressure" and "stresses" of everyday life. This suggests for both speakers, thinking and being in nature provides an escape from the challenges of life.

AO3 — relate the poems to the context

- Although both poems present the natural world as an escape, the contexts they were written in are very different. For Wordsworth, 'Lines Written in Early Spring', explores how everything is in harmony in the natural world, yet humans treat each other with unkindness. His poem could be a criticism of society at the time, including the violence of the French Revolution, and the suffering and environmental damage caused by the Industrial Revolution. On the other hand, Robinson's 'A Portable Paradise', explores ideas of belonging and a yearning for home, as the paradise he describes shares similarities with his childhood home of Trinidad.

This answer should be marked in accordance with the levels-based mark scheme on page 134.

Make sure your answer to this question is in paragraphs and full sentences. Bullet points have been used in this example answer to suggest some information you could include.

We've included some quotes from *A Portable Paradise* (**page 106**) in this sample answer, but direct quotes from the comparison poem aren't essential; you can use paraphrased examples or summaries to demonstrate your understanding.

ENGLAND IN 1819
— PERCY BYSSHE SHELLEY

The monarchy is presented as being disinterested in the suffering of the English people.

The consonance of the repeated 'd' sound mimics the speaker angrily spitting out these words.

Using the present tense makes the poem seem more immediate and urgent.

The monarchy is described as a "*muddy spring*", which suggests it is tainted.

An old, mad, blind, despised, and dying King;
Princes, the dregs of their dull race, who flow
Through public scorn,—mud from a muddy spring;
Rulers who neither see nor feel nor know,
5   But leechlike to their fainting country cling
Till they drop, blind in blood, without a blow.
A people starved and stabbed in th' untilled field;
An army, whom liberticide and prey
Makes as a two-edged sword to all who wield;
10 Golden and sanguine laws which tempt and slay;
Religion Christless, Godless—a book sealed;
A senate, Time's worst statute, unrepealed—
Are graves from which a glorious Phantom may
Burst, to illumine our tempestuous day.

Comparing the monarchy to leeches creates an unpleasant image.

Ordinary English people are presented as victims of the monarchy, oppressed by starvation and violence.

"*Golden*" implies the lawmakers are bribed. "*sanguine*" can mean 'blood-red' which suggests the laws result in bloodshed and suffering.

Caesura interrupts the flow of the poem, and reinforces the speaker's anger.

The first twelve lines focus on the problems facing England, emphasising how widespread and overwhelming the issues are.

"*may*" introduces possibility: England's revival isn't guaranteed.

"*Burst*" is positioned at the start of the line to give it emphasis.

The image of sunlight shining through dark clouds ends the poem on a hopeful note.

> **?** **liberticide** — destroyer of freedom   **sanguine** — positive, or blood-red
> **senate** — a group of politicians with the power to make laws
> **statute** — an officially recognised law   **illumine** — illuminate, brighten
> **tempestuous** — chaotic

18   ClearRevise

Percy Bysshe Shelley

Percy Bysshe Shelley (1792–1822) was an English **Romantic** poet (see **page 11**). Shelley was politically radical: he was against the monarchy and was an atheist (someone who doesn't believe in the existence of God). His beliefs were controversial at the time.

In 1818, Shelley left England for Italy. His move was partly health-related (doctors believed that warmer weather would improve Shelley's poor health) but he also wanted to escape the "tyranny" of England. *England in 1819* wasn't published until 1839, seventeen years after his death.

> **Comment:** If *England in 1819* had been published during his lifetime, it's likely Shelley would have been imprisoned (or possibly executed) for treason (criticising the monarchy).

Percy Bysshe Shelley

Summary of the poem

The speaker describes the state of England in 1819. England is ruled by a "*old, mad*" king, and the rest of the royal family are unpopular. The monarchy doesn't seem to know or care about the difficulties faced by ordinary people. The army destroys freedom, rather than protecting it, and religious leaders are corrupt and "*Christless*". However, the speaker is hopeful that these powerful institutions will collapse, and a new, "*glorious*" England will emerge.

Context and references

The Peterloo Massacre

In the 1810s, Britain experienced bad harvests, high levels of unemployment and high prices for basic goods, such as bread. This meant that many ordinary people suffered.

> **Comment:** This is reflected in the speaker describing British people as "*starved*" and England as "*fainting*".

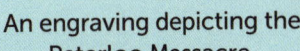
An engraving depicting the Peterloo Massacre.

Ordinary people hoped to bring about change through Parliamentary reform. At the time, only 11% of men were eligible to vote, and those who could vote belonged to the wealthiest groups in society. Reformers hoped that by allowing all men the right to vote, Parliament would become fairer and more representative of society. However, Parliament refused to consider any changes.

In August 1819, reformers in Manchester organised a rally in St Peter's Field to campaign for more widespread voting rights, and over 60,000 people attended. However, armed men on horseback were instructed to ride into the crowd to break up the rally and arrest the ringleaders. The charge resulted in the deaths of approximately 15 people, and hundreds more were injured. Newspapers dubbed the event 'The Peterloo Massacre' (a reference to the bloody Battle of Waterloo which had happened several years earlier).

> **Comment:** The speaker accuses the army of "*liberticide*", the destruction of freedom.

Context continued

King George III

King George III (1738–1820) ruled during Shelley's lifetime. For the last 10 years of his reign, King George was blind, deaf, and mentally incapable of running the country.

King George III

Comment: Shelley wrote *England in 1819* just before King George's death in 1820. George is the "*old, mad, blind, despised, and dying King*" described in the opening line.

George's son, Prince George, acted as regent (someone who rules when the monarch is unable to). Prince George's extravagant lifestyle made him unpopular with the ordinary British people who suffered under his rule.

Comment: Prince George is described as "*mud from a muddy spring*", which suggests the speaker felt the whole royal family was corrupt.

Themes

Oppression

British people are presented as being oppressed by powerful institutions such as the monarchy, army and Church.

Form and structure

The poem is loosely based on a **sonnet** structure.

Comment: Sonnets are always 14 lines long, and are usually categorised as either **Shakespearian** or **Petrarchan sonnets**.
- A Shakespearian sonnet is divided into three quatrains, and ends with a rhyming couplet.
- A Petrarchan sonnet is made up of an octave (eight lines) with an ABBAABBA rhyme scheme, followed by a sestet (six lines) with either a CDCDCD or CDECDE rhyme scheme. The sestet usually begins with a **volta** (turning point).

England in 1819 opens with a sestet with an ABABAB rhyme scheme, followed by a quatrain with a CDCD rhyme scheme, and ends with two couplets. The poem doesn't exactly follow the structure of either a Shakespearian or Petrarchan sonnet, so its unexpected rhyme scheme could reflect the unequal nature of English society, and the discontent it causes.

Comment: Sonnets were typically used for love poetry. Shelley may have used the sonnet form to suggest the love he feels for his country.

Form and structure continued

The first twelve lines of the poem focus on the issues affecting England. The list of problems seems endless which suggests how overwhelming the issues are, and how they preoccupy the speaker.

> **Comment:** The poem uses lots of **caesura**, which creates a choppy, disjointed rhythm. This suggests that the speaker is so angry about the state of England that his thoughts are wild and uncontrollable.

However, there is a **volta** on line 13, and the speaker's tone changes. The poem concludes with the speaker seeming more hopeful about England's future.

> **Comment:** The speaker suggests that things "*may*" improve. This **modal verb** introduces possibility, not certainty, warning that England's revival is not guaranteed.

Tone

The poem has an angry tone. The speaker resents powerful institutions that oppress ordinary people.

> **Comment:** The speaker uses unpleasant language and imagery to describe the monarchy, such as "*dregs*", "*mud*" and "*leechlike*" to reinforce his contempt.

Much of the poem has a pessimistic tone: the situation in England seems beyond hope.

> **Comment:** Even though the public "*scorn*" the monarchy, they are powerless to improve their situation.

The speaker suggests that a "*glorious Phantom*" (see **page 23**) could save England. This ends the poem on a more optimistic note.

Language

Representation of England and its people

Weak

England is **personified** as "*fainting*". This suggests that it has been weakened by the "*leechlike*" rulers who have sucked all the strength from it.

Oppressed

The speaker uses violent language such as "*blood*", "*blow*", "*stabbed*" and "*slay*" to suggest that English people are oppressed by violence.

Impoverished

Ordinary English people are described as "*starved*" and their fields are "*untilled*". This could refer to the economic hardships that England faced following bad harvests in the 1810s.

Language

Representation of authority

Monarchy

- The king is described as "*old, mad, blind, despised and dying*" which reflects the speaker's contempt towards the monarchy. The repeated **plosive** sounds ('b' and 'd') suggests the speaker spits out the words angrily. The word "*blind*" likely refers to King George's poor vision, but also suggests that he's 'blind' to the problems affecting England.
- The speaker uses the **metaphor** "*muddy spring*" to describe the royal family. Usually a spring (source of water) symbolises hope and purity, but the adjective "*muddy*" implies that the monarchy is tainted.
- The speaker describes how the monarchy "*neither see nor feel nor know*". This suggests the royal family are out of touch with ordinary people and have no interest in the hardships they face.

Comment: The speaker uses a **triplet** (sometimes called a 'list of three') in the phrase "*neither see nor feel nor know*". This technique helps to emphasise the monarchy's disinterest towards the English people.

- The speaker uses an **extended metaphor** to compare the royal family to leeches. Leeches are worm-like creatures which attach to other animals and suck blood from them. Likening the royal family to leeches dehumanises them, and suggests that they feed off the country, and give nothing in return.

Comment: The speaker describes how they "*cling / Till they drop, blind in blood, without a blow*". The **alliteration** of the 'b' sound in "*blind in blood*" and "*blow*" reinforces the unpleasant image of fat, swollen leeches.

Army

The army are accused of "*liberticide*" (destroying freedom). This could refer to the Peterloo Massacre where ordinary people were killed during a peaceful rally.

Parliament

Parliament is described as passing "*Golden*" laws. Although gold often has positive connotations, here "*Golden*" suggests that politicians are corrupt: they make laws which make themselves rich, or accept bribes from powerful individuals. The speaker also describes "*sanguine laws*". 'Sanguine' can mean 'the colour of blood'. This hints that Parliament's laws often lead to bloodshed.

Language continued

Representation of authority continued

Church

The Church is described as *"Christless, Godless"*, suggesting that religious leaders do not follow the example set by God or Jesus. Instead, they exploit people's religious faith for their own benefit.

The phrase *"a book sealed"* likely refers to the Bible. This could suggest that religious leaders ignore the teachings of the Bible, and do not treat people with kindness and compassion.

Comment: The speaker suggests that all the powerful institutions in England are corrupt and greedy. This implies that ordinary English people have no one to turn to for help.

The *"glorious Phantom"*

In the final couplet, the speaker refers to a *"glorious Phantom"*. This could have several meanings:

- It could be the spirit of England which will rise again after the collapse of the monarchy, Church and Parliament.
- It could be a new power structure which will replace the old, corrupt institutions.
- It could be freedom for the English people following a revolution.

Comment: Inspired by the French Revolution (see **page 11**), Shelley may be calling on people to revolt, and overthrow corrupt officials.

A phoenix

The *"glorious Phantom"* has similarities with a phoenix rising from the ashes. This suggests that England will be able to renew itself and come back stronger than before.

> Phoenixes are mythological birds with fiery tail feathers which burn themselves to death and are born again from the ashes. Phoenixes symbolise regeneration.

The *"glorious Phantom"* might *"illumine our tempestuous day"*. The phrase *"tempestuous day"* refers to stormy, violent weather, and represents the chaotic situation in England at the time.

Comment: The plural determiner *"our"* in the phrase *"our tempestuous day"* includes the speaker in the suffering of the English people, which helps him connect with the reader.

However, the word *"illumine"* creates an image of sunlight breaking through dark clouds, and ends the poem with a sense of hope and optimism.

COMPARING *ENGLAND IN 1819*

Here's how *England in 1819* could be compared to other poems.

 Remember, you can compare *England in 1819* with any poem from the anthology as long as your response is supported with examples. The following examples suggest ways to compare the poems, but they are not complete answers.

Angry tone

England in 1819 is critical of powerful institutions, such as the monarchy, army and Parliament. The speaker uses negative language such as "*An old, mad, blind, despised, and dying King*" to show his contempt for the monarchy, and the repetition of plosive sounds such as 'b' and 'd' create the impression that the speaker is spitting out these words angrily. This angry tone is reinforced by the speaker's use of caesura. The caesura creates a choppy, disjointed rhythm which interrupts the flow of the poem, and suggests that the speaker cannot contain his rage towards the powerful institutions which oppress ordinary English people.

Just like *England in 1819*, the speaker in *pot* (**page 58**) is also critical of powerful institutions. In this poem, the speaker criticises museums and the British government for stealing artefacts from other countries and not returning them. In the poem, the speaker talks directly to a pot which was stolen from Nigeria by colonialists and is now on display in a museum in Manchester. The speaker wants to "*shatter*" the glass case the pot is displayed in and return it to Nigeria. The word "*shatter*" has connotations of a violent, forceful act, which highlights the speaker's anger.

Attitudes towards law enforcement

England in 1819 suggests that English people are oppressed by the powerful institutions which are supposed to protect them, such as the army. The speaker describes how English people are "*stabbed*", and this violent word could refer to the Peterloo Massacre, where a peaceful demonstration about voting rights turned deadly when men on horseback rode through the crowd. The speaker reinforces this criticism of law enforcement by accusing the army of "*liberticide*", implying that they destroy freedom, rather than protect it.

Thirteen (**page 122**) is also critical of institutions which claim to protect the public, specifically the police force. The speaker recalls how he was apprehended by police when he was 13 years old. He uses the word "*cornered*" to reflect how the police officers used their power and authority to make him feel powerless and vulnerable. The police officers are so threatening that "*fear condenses*" on the speaker's lip, suggesting that the speaker begins to sweat because he is so afraid of what the police may do to him.

Compare how poets present ideas about oppression in *England in 1819* and in **one** other poem from Worlds and Lives. [30 marks]

Your answer may include:

AO1 — show understanding of the poems

- 'England in 1819' criticises how English people were oppressed by powerful institutions in the early 19th century. 'A century later' explores how some girls are oppressed by those who want to prevent girls from receiving an education.

AO2 — show understanding of the poets' language choices

- Both speakers use violent language to vividly describe the reality of oppression. In 'England in 1819', the speaker uses the words "starved", "stabbed" and "slay" to describe how the English people suffer. The brutality of the words also implies how difficult it is for English people to stand up against their oppressors. In 'A century later', the speaker describes how the schoolgirl "takes the bullet in the head". This blunt statement is shocking, and reinforces the senseless violence used to try to oppress the girl.

- Both speakers use the present tense. This makes the suffering of the English people in 'England in 1819' and the schoolgirls in 'A century later' seem more immediate, and reminds the reader that the oppression they face is on-going.

- Both speakers end their poems with a hopeful, but uncertain, image, which suggests that people can overcome oppression but it is not guaranteed. In 'England in 1819', the speaker describes a "glorious Phantom" which "may... / ... illumine our tempestuous day". This could represent the spirit of England which will rise again following a revolution. The word "illumine" suggests a strong, powerful light, and may remind the reader of sunlight breaking through clouds following a storm. However, the word "may" indicates possibility, rather than certainty, which suggests that England's revival is not guaranteed. Similarly, in 'A century later', the final image is of "schoolgirls" taking "their places on the front line". This suggests the defiance of young girls who will continue to fight for their right to education. However, the connotations of "front line" hints that the girls are putting themselves at risk.

AO3 — relate the poems to the context

- Both poems are based on real-life examples of oppression. 'England in 1819' was inspired by the Peterloo Massacre, where innocent people were killed during a rally for voting rights. 'A century later' is based on the experience of Malala Yousafzai, a Pakistani schoolgirl who was shot in the head because she was vocal about girls' right to education. Both speakers may have wanted to inspire readers to take action against oppression.

This answer should be marked in accordance with the levels-based mark scheme on page 134.

Make sure your answer to this question is in paragraphs and full sentences. Bullet points have been used in this example answer to suggest some information you could include.

We've included some quotes from *A century later* (**page 82**) in this sample answer, but direct quotes from the comparison poem aren't essential; you can use paraphrased examples or summaries to demonstrate your understanding.

SHALL EARTH NO MORE INSPIRE THEE — EMILY BRONTË

The speaker opens with two rhetorical questions, and uses the following stanzas to persuade the subject to fall back in love with nature.

The speaker uses imperative verbs to command the subject and create an authoritative tone.

Repetition of "*I know*" reinforces the omniscient nature of the speaker.

"*sunshine*" contrasts with "*regions dark*" in the previous stanza, suggesting that nature is the solution to the subject's sadness.

Shall earth no more inspire thee,
Thou lonely dreamer now?
Since passion may not fire thee
Shall Nature cease to bow?

5 Thy mind is ever moving
In regions dark to thee;
Recall its useless roving—
Come back and dwell with me.

I know my mountain breezes
10 Enchant and soothe thee still—
I know my sunshine pleases
Despite thy wayward will.

When day with evening blending
Sinks from the summer sky,
15 I've seen thy spirit bending
In fond idolatry.

The speaker addresses an unknown subject using second person archaic (old fashioned) pronouns.

The subject has "*dark*" thoughts, suggesting they are troubled.

"*useless*" suggests the subject worries unnecessarily.

Sensory language presents nature as soothing.

The positive verbs "*Enchant*", "*soothe*" and "*pleases*" reinforce the healing power of nature.

The sibilance in this line is soft and calming which matches the peaceful mood of the stanza.

"*spirit*" and "*idolatry*" have religious connotations which reflect the spiritual connection between the subject and nature. This could also suggest that the speaker is God.

> I've watched thee every hour;
> I know my mighty sway,
> I know my magic power
> 20 To drive thy griefs away.
>
> Few hearts to mortals given
> On earth so wildly pine;
> Yet none would ask a heaven
> More like this earth than thine.
>
> 25 Then let my winds caress thee;
> Thy comrade let me be—
> Since nought beside can bless thee,
> Return and dwell with me.

Annotations:

- This stanza focuses on the omniscience and power of the speaker, hinting that the speaker could be Earth, Nature or God. *(I know my magic power)*
- "*Few hearts*" suggests that the subject's sensitivity is uncommon, and others may struggle to understand the depth of their emotions.
- The speaker believes that nature creates heaven on earth. *(Yet none would ask a heaven / More like this earth than thine.)*
- "*caress*" is a gentle, loving gesture, which suggests that the speaker cares about the subject.
- The speaker uses everyday examples of nature, such as the wind, sunshine and sunsets. These would be recognisable for most readers, allowing them to reflect on their own experiences of nature.
- The final line is a command, and the reader hopes that the subject will be reinspired by nature.

?
- **fire** — motivate
- **roving** — constantly moving
- **wayward** — disobedient
- **idolatry** — devotion
- **pine** — long for
- **comrade** — friend

GCSE English Literature Poetry Anthology | Worlds and Lives

Emily Brontë

Emily Brontë (1818–1848) was an English novelist and poet who was inspired by the **Romantic movement** (see below). She spent much of her life in Yorkshire, and was inspired by the local landscape. *Shall earth no more inspire thee* was written in 1841, and published in 1850 after her death.

Emily Brontë

Summary of the poem

The speaker addresses someone who no longer enjoys nature because they are overcome with sadness. The speaker encourages them to reconnect with nature to "*drive thy griefs away*".

Comment: The subject of the poem could be Brontë herself. She was known to be very reclusive and solitary, but loved spending time in nature.

Context and references

Romantic movement

Shall earth no more inspire thee contains features often found in Romantic literature.

 Romantic literature often explored extreme emotions. → The subject has "*dark*" thoughts and is overcome by "*griefs*".

 Romantic literature often explored the beauty and power of nature. → The poem presents nature as beautiful, but also powerful and restorative.

 The Romantic movement believed in **individualism**: the power and worth of the individual. → The speaker (assumed to be Nature) is dismayed that an individual has lost enthusiasm for nature, and uses the poem to try to inspire them.

Themes

Nature

The poem focuses on nature's ability to bring joy into someone's life.

Spirituality & religion

The speaker suggests that connecting with nature can be a spiritual experience.

Loneliness

The subject is a "*lonely dreamer*", who is disconnected from the world around them. They may feel isolated because their emotional sensitivity is uncommon ("*Few hearts*" feel as deeply as they do), so others struggle to understand them.

Form and structure

Shall earth no more inspire thee is an example of a **persona poem**, where the poet has assumed someone else's identity. The speaker in the poem is omniscient (all-knowing) and powerful ("*I've watched thee every hour; / I know my mighty sway*"). It's not clear who the speaker is, but it could be God, nature or Earth (for more on the speaker, see **page 30**).

The poem shares some features with **dramatic monologues**, where the speaker addresses an unknown subject. The subject could be interpreted as an individual, humanity or the poet herself.

Archaic language

The speaker addresses the subject using second-person pronouns that had largely fallen out of use by the time the poem was written: "*thy*" which means 'your', "*thee*" which means 'you' and "*thine*" which means 'yours'. Although these pronouns weren't often used in everyday speech and writing in the 1800s, they could be found in poems, as they were considered more literary and more romantic than 'you' and 'your'.

The poem is divided into seven quatrains, and the first six use a regular ABAB rhyme scheme. This regular structure could reflect the peace and harmony found in nature. However, the final quatrain switches to an AAAA rhyme scheme.

Comment: The change in the rhyme scheme in the final stanza could represent the unity the speaker hopes to achieve with the subject.

In each stanza, the first and third lines contain seven syllables, and the second and fourth lines have six. This regular rhythm creates a steady pace, which matches the speaker's calm tone.

Comment: The exception to this is the fifth stanza, where all the lines have six syllables. This could reflect the speaker's determination to help the subject.

The poem opens with two **rhetorical questions**, asking whether the subject has lost interest in nature. The following six stanzas attempt to persuade the subject to fall back in love with nature.

Tone

The poem has a calm tone, reinforced by the regular rhythm and rhyme scheme. The speaker reassures the subject, and reminds them about the beauty of nature.

The speaker uses a persuasive tone. They use rhetorical questions, imperative verbs and repetition to try to convince the subject to appreciate the beauty of nature.

Language

Representation of the speaker

Powerful

The speaker has a "*mighty sway*" and "*magic power*".

Comment: The speaker can control the "*mountain breezes*" and "*sunshine*", so could be interpreted as God, Earth or nature.

Watchful

The speaker is omnipresent (everywhere at once), commenting "*I've watched thee every hour*". This reinforces the idea that the speaker is a supernatural force.

Perceptive

The speaker uses **anaphora**, repeating the phrase "*I know*". This suggests they are perceptive.

Comment: The speaker states "*I know my mountain breezes / Enchant and soothe thee still*". This suggests that the speaker knows the subject better than they know themself.

Compassionate

The speaker cares about the subject, and wants them to be happy. The speaker hopes that by reminding them about the beauty of nature, they can "*drive*" away the subject's sadness.

Representation of nature

Nature is **personified** in the line: "*Shall Nature cease to bow?*", which compares nature to an actor who entertains the subject, bowing at the end of the performance. This implies that nature exists for the pleasure of humans.

The speaker believes that the subject will be happy again if they can reconnect with nature, so they describe pleasant scenes such as "*mountain breezes*", "*sunshine*" and a sunset to remind the subject of nature's beauty. Readers will be familiar with these images and sensations, which may inspire them to draw on their own experiences of nature when reading the poem.

Comment: The **sibilance** in the phrase "*Sinks from the summer sky*" makes the line sound hushed and soothing, which reflects the calming nature of the sunset.

Language continued

Representation of the subject

Reclusive

The subject is described as a "*lonely dreamer*" which implies they spend time alone, lost in their thoughts.

Comment: Brontë had few friends outside of her family, so she may have identified with someone who was "*lonely*".

Sad

The speaker thinks about "*dark*" things, and is overcome with "*griefs*".

Uninspired

The subject's low mood has caused them to lose interest in nature.

Imaginative

The subject is described as a "*dreamer*" whose "*mind is ever moving*" which suggests they have a vivid imagination.

Stubborn

The subject has a "*wayward will*" which implies they can be reluctant to change their mind.

Religious language

The speaker uses religious language throughout the poem, such as "*spirit*", "*idolatry*", "*heaven*" and "*bless*". This reinforces the idea that connecting with nature can be a spiritual experience.

Comment: The religious language could hint that the speaker is God.

Persuasive language

The speaker uses persuasive techniques to try to convince the subject to find joy in nature:

Rhetorical questions

The first stanza is made up of two **rhetorical questions** which encourage the subject to reflect on their attitude towards nature.

Imperative verbs

The speaker uses **imperative verbs** to command the subject, such as "*Come back*", "*dwell*" and "*Return*".

Repetition

The speaker repeats the phrase "*I know*" which makes them seem confident and reassuring.

Positive verbs

The speaker uses joyful verbs such as "*Enchant*", "*soothe*" and "*pleases*" to remind the subject of the positive impact nature can have on their mood.

COMPARING *SHALL EARTH NO MORE INSPIRE THEE*

Here's how *Shall earth no more inspire thee* could be compared to other poems.

Remember, you can compare *Shall earth no more inspire thee* with any poem from the anthology as long as your response is supported with examples. The following examples suggest ways to compare the poems, but they are not complete answers.

The healing power of nature

In *Shall earth no more inspire thee*, nature is presented as a comforting and restorative force that can distract someone from sadness. The subject of the poem has "*dark*" thoughts, which could imply they are suffering from depression. The speaker, who could be interpreted as nature, describes how breezes "*soothe*", sunshine "*pleases*" and winds "*caress*" the subject to make them feel more positive. These reassuring verbs suggest that nature uses its power to comfort humans.

In *Lines Written in Early Spring* (**page 10**), nature is also presented as a comforting force that can distract humans from "*sad thoughts*". The speaker sits "*reclined*" listening to birdsong, which encourages him to think "*pleasant thoughts*". The word "*reclined*" suggests that the speaker is relaxed and at peace. Like the subject in *Shall earth no more inspire thee*, the speaker in *Lines Written in Early Spring* is in a sad mood, suggested by the words "*grieved*" and "*lament*". However, the speaker finds pleasure watching the "*budding twigs*" and "*primrose tufts*", suggesting that nature has the power to bring joy. Both Brontë and Wordsworth were Romantic poets, and the Romantic movement often used literature to explore the power of nature.

Feelings of disconnection

The subject in *Shall earth no more inspire thee* seems to struggle to connect with the world around her. She is described as a "*lonely dreamer*" who is experiencing "*griefs*". This suggests that she feels isolated, and this disconnection makes her feel sad. The subject's solitary nature is reinforced by the phrase "*Few hearts.../ ... so wildly pine*", which suggests that few people can empathise with the subject's intense emotions. However, the speaker offers the subject companionship, by asking to be their "*comrade*", and urging them to "*Return and dwell with me*". This gives the reader hope that the subject will be able to reconnect with the world around her.

The speaker in *In a London Drawingroom* (**page 34**) also appears to struggle with feelings of loneliness and disconnection. She describes how people in London "*glance unmarking at the passers by*". The verb "*glance*" implies that Londoners quickly look away from each other and the word "*unmarking*" suggests that they are disinterested in the people around them. This suggests that London is an unfriendly and isolating place to live. Unlike *Shall earth no more inspire thee*, there is little hope that the speaker will be able to connect with the world around her, as the poem ends with a pessimistic tone when the speaker reflects on the lack of "*warmth & joy*" in London.

Compare how poets present ideas about nature in *Shall earth no more inspire thee* and in **one** other poem from Worlds and Lives. [30 marks]

Your answer may include:

AO1 — show understanding of the poems

- Both 'Shall earth no more inspire thee' and 'With Birds You're Never Lonely' explore the idea that surrounding yourself with the beauty of nature can bring peace, as well as provide an escape from the difficulties of life. In both poems, nature is also presented as a companion for anyone struggling with loneliness.

AO2 — show understanding of the poets' language choices

- Both poems present nature as beautiful. In 'Shall earth no more inspire thee', the speaker uses imagery to describe a beautiful sunset. Sibilance in the phrase "Sinks from the summer sky" repeats the soft, hushed 's' sound which matches the calm beauty of a sunset. In 'With Birds You're Never Lonely', the speaker also uses sibilance and light imagery to describe the beauty of nature. The phrase "sun-syrupped Kauri trees" creates an image of trees glowing with light.

- Both poems describe individuals who struggle to connect with the world around them, but find comfort in nature. In 'Shall earth no more inspire thee', the subject is described as a "lonely dreamer", which suggests that they struggle to relate to others. However, the speaker, who could be interpreted as nature, wants to be the subject's "comrade", suggesting that nature can provide companionship. Similarly, in 'With Birds You're Never Lonely', the speaker is "alone" in the forest, which suggests he feels disconnected from other people. However, he is soon surrounded by birds, and later includes the line "with birds you're never lonely", which suggests that being in nature helps him feel less alone.

- Both poems reflect on humans' relationship with nature. In 'Shall earth no more inspire thee', the speaker uses the rhetorical question "Shall Nature cease to bow?". This question personifies nature as an actor who 'performs' to entertain humans. This reminds the reader how humankind benefits from nature. Similarly, in 'With Birds You're Never Lonely', the speaker includes the rhetorical question, "What books would they write if they had to cut us down?". The speaker personifies trees, and reminds the reader of the damage humans do to the environment, when we cut down trees to make paper for our own benefit.

AO3 — relate the poems to the context

- Both poets may have drawn on their own experiences of isolation and feelings of disconnection to inspire their poems. Brontë was reported to be very introverted and reclusive, so she could be the "lonely dreamer" in 'Shall earth no more inspire thee'. Similarly, Antrobus is deaf, and his poetry often explores ideas around connection. In the opening line of 'With Birds You're Never Lonely', he "can't hear the barista", which highlights the additional challenges his deafness can cause when trying to connect with others.

This answer should be marked in accordance with the levels-based mark scheme on page 134.

Make sure your answer to this question is in paragraphs and full sentences. Bullet points have been used in this example answer to suggest some information you could include.

We've included some quotes from *With Birds You're Never Lonely* (**pages 98–99**) in this sample answer, but direct quotes from the comparison poem aren't essential; you can use paraphrased examples or summaries to demonstrate your understanding.

IN A LONDON DRAWINGROOM — GEORGE ELIOT

The poem is a single, unbroken stanza. This could reflect how the speaker is overwhelmed by London.

"Cutting" is a vicious word, which hints at humankind's negative impact on the world.

This metaphor suggests that sunlight cannot break through the pollution, reinforcing how thick it is.

The "closed" carriages suggest that Londoners are shut off from each other.

The sky is cloudy, yellowed by the smoke.
For view there are the houses opposite
Cutting the sky with one long line of wall
Like solid fog: far as the eye can stretch
5 Monotony of surface & of form
Without a break to hang a guess upon.
No bird can make a shadow as it flies,
For all is shadow, as in ways o'erhung
By thickest canvass, where the golden rays
10 Are clothed in hemp. No figure lingering
Pauses to feed the hunger of the eye
Or rest a little on the lap of life.
All hurry on & look upon the ground,
Or glance unmarking at the passers by
15 The wheels are hurrying too, cabs, carriages
All closed, in multiplied identity.
The world seems one huge prison-house & court
Where men are punished at the slightest cost,
With lowest rate of colour, warmth & joy.

This hints at the pollution caused by the Industrial Revolution

This implies the view doesn't inspire wonder or imagination.

Repetition of "shadow" reinforces the gloomy scene.

Alliteration of the soft 'l' sound reinforces the joy a slower pace of life can bring.

Enjambment mimics the hurried movement of the people outside.

The simile suggests that Londoners feel trapped.

The triplet in the closing line reinforces the miserable tone of the poem, and doesn't suggest things will improve.

? **hemp** — a coarse fabric
o'erhung — overhung, covered with

George Eliot

George Eliot (1819–1880) was the pen name of novelist and poet Mary Ann Evans.

Comment: Evans wrote under a male name because she thought she would be taken more seriously as a writer if readers thought she was a man.

She was born on a country estate outside of Nuneaton, a small town in the Midlands. She moved to London in 1850 and wrote *In a London Drawingroom* in 1865.

Comment: Eliot grew up in a rural area, so the poem could reflect her dissatisfaction towards living in a large city.

George Eliot

Summary of the poem

The speaker is sitting in a drawingroom (lounge) looking out of a window at a street in London. The view is gloomy and clouded by smoke, and the people who pass by seem rushed and miserable. The speaker compares living in London to a punishment.

Context and references

The Industrial Revolution

The Industrial Revolution (see **page 11**) was made possible because of the development of steam power. Factories burnt coal to create steam which powered machinery. However, burning fuel contributed to rising pollution levels which negatively impacted people's health and the environment.

Skyline of Victorian London and coal-burning chimneys.

Comment: In the poem, the sky is *"yellowed by the smoke"*.

The Industrial Revolution also contributed to the problem of overdevelopment, where too many buildings were constructed in a small area.

Comment: The speaker hints at the problem of overdevelopment by describing a row of houses as *"solid fog"*, suggesting that the buildings block light from reaching the city.

Themes

Environmental damage

London is negatively impacted by air pollution and overdevelopment, but only the speaker seems to care.

Loneliness

Londoners are presented as being disconnected from each other.

Nature

Nature struggles to survive in the dark and gloomy city, as sunlight can't break through the air pollution.

Form and structure

Comment: The speaker's identity is unknown, but it could be Eliot herself since she was living in London when the poem was written.

In a London Drawingroom is written as a single, unbroken stanza. This could reflect how life in the city overwhelms the speaker.

Comment: The unbroken stanza could also reflect the lack of space in London due to overdevelopment and urbanisation.

The poem is written in **blank verse**: there is no rhyme scheme, but the lines are written in **iambic pentameter** (10 syllables per line, in a pattern of unstressed, followed by stressed). Iambic pentameter closely matches the pattern of natural speech which reinforces the voice of the speaker.

Comment: The lack of rhyme scheme contributes to the joyless, dreary tone of the poem. It could also reflect how the speaker doesn't feel as though she belongs in London.

The speaker uses **enjambment** throughout which quickens the pace of the poem and mimics the rushed, relentless movement of Londoners "*hurrying*" by.

Much of the poem describes the dreary scene the speaker sees out of the window, and it ends with a **triplet** (list of three) stating that London has the "*lowest rate of colour, warmth & joy*". This reinforces the poem's pessimistic tone, and leaves the reader with the impression that there is little happiness to be found in the city.

Tone

The poem has a miserable tone. The speaker is disillusioned by the high levels of pollution, the uninspiring view and the unsociable attitude of Londoners.

The poem ends with a sense of hopelessness, suggesting that things won't improve.

Comment: The speaker seems lonely. She struggles to connect with London and the people living in it.

Language

Representation of nature

The speaker criticises urbanisation by describing its negative impact on nature.

- The speaker uses a **metaphor** to describe the houses *"Cutting the sky"*. The violent connotations of *"Cutting"* suggest that overdevelopment and urbanisation are damaging the environment.
- The phrase *"No bird can make a shadow"* suggests that sunlight cannot break through the smoke, and nature lives in darkness.

Comment: The speaker repeats *"shadow"* which emphasises the dark and gloomy scene.

- The sun's *"golden rays / Are clothed in hemp"*. This **metaphor** reinforces how sunlight is blocked out by the thick air pollution.

Comment: Hemp was made into fabric in factories in the 19th century, so the speaker may be criticising the textile industry's negative impact on the environment.

GCSE English Literature Poetry Anthology | Worlds and Lives

Language continued

Description of pollution

The speaker suggests that air pollution has made London gloomy and dirty.

- The sky is "*yellowed by the smoke*", which suggests the air is noxious and unpleasant.
- A row of houses is described using the **simile** "*Like solid fog*", implying that even the buildings merge into the gloom of the city.
- "*For all is shadow*" suggests a thick layer of pollution hangs over London.

Comment: The speaker's description of London makes the pollution seem inescapable and suffocating. This adds to the sense of confinement in the poem (see **below**).

Language of confinement

The speaker uses language associated with confinement to suggest how trapped she feels.

Comment: Overdevelopment often leads to overcrowding so the speaker may feel restricted by the lack of space in London.

 The houses are described as "*one long line of wall*", hinting that the speaker sees them as a barrier.

 The carriages are "*All closed*", which suggests that Londoners shut each other out.

 London is compared to a "*prison-house*", which implies that living in the city feels like an inescapable punishment. Prisons in the 19th century were often overcrowded, so the speaker may also be commenting on how claustrophobic the city makes her feel.

Language continued

Representation of London and Londoners

Monotonous

Houses are described as having "*Monotony of surface and form*", suggesting they all look alike. Londoners have a "*multiplied identity*", implying a lack of individuality.

Uncaring

Londoners "*glance unmarking at the passers by*". "*glance*" suggests they quickly look away, and the word "*unmarking*" suggests they do not care.

Uninspired

Londoners see nothing to "*feed the hunger of the eye*", which suggests that nothing in the city inspires them or brings them joy.

Comment: The words "*feed*" and "*hunger*" suggest that the speaker believes inspiration and joy are just as important as food.

Unpleasant

The city is described as having the "*lowest rate of colour, warmth & joy*", which suggests it is an unwelcoming place.

Comment: The speaker presents London in an overwhelmingly negative way which suggests she doesn't feel as though she belongs in London.

Rushed

Londoners "*hurry*" and the carriages are "*hurrying*". The speaker remarks how Londoners do not seem to stop to appreciate life.

Comment: The speaker comments that "*No figure... / Pauses*" and "*All hurry*". This suggests that everyone is in a rush, and the busyness is inescapable.

Judgemental

London is also described as a "*court*", which implies that people in the city judge each other.

COMPARING *IN A LONDON DRAWINGROOM*

Here's how *In a London Drawingroom* could be compared to other poems.

 Remember, you can compare *In a London Drawingroom* with any poem from the anthology as long as your response is supported with examples. The following examples suggest ways to compare the poems, but they are not complete answers.

Suffering

In a London Drawingroom presents London as an unpleasant city that is full of suffering. The speaker compares London to "*one huge prison-house*", and this simile suggests that living in London is an inescapable punishment. This is reinforced with the description that Londoners are "*punished… / With lowest rate of colour, warmth & joy*". This triplet emphasises how unpleasant London seems to the speaker, and how much the people who live there must suffer.

The speaker in *England in 1819* (**page 18**) presents the English public as suffering at the hands of corrupt authorities. England is personified as "*fainting*", which suggests that the country has been weakened by the "*leechlike*" rulers who feed off it. The suffering of the English public is reinforced by the description of people being "*starved and stabbed*". The sibilance creates an unpleasant hissing sound, and reflects the contempt felt by the speaker towards the corrupt authorities who oppress English people.

Loneliness in cities

In a London Drawingroom explores how isolated the speaker feels in London. She describes how Londoners "*hurry on & look upon the ground*" and "*glance unmarking at passers by*". These lines suggest that Londoners are too busy with their own lives to make connections with people around them. This is reinforced by the description of the carriages being "*closed*", which suggests that people in the city are guarded and unwilling to reach out to others. The speaker finds this lack of connection isolating, and suggests that she feels unwelcome in London.

The speaker in *With Birds You're Never Lonely* (**page 98**) also suggests that people in London are disconnected from each other. He describes a man "*sitting in the corner / of the café reading alone*". Sitting in "*the corner*" "*alone*" suggests the man has tucked himself away, and doesn't want to be disturbed. This suggests that city life can be isolating for some people. However, the speaker catches the man's eye, which implies the speaker empathises with the man, and wants to make a connection. This reinforces the importance of reaching out to people to help them feel less lonely.

Compare how poets present feelings about place in *In a London Drawingroom* and in **one** other poem from Worlds and Lives. [30 marks]

Your answer may include:

AO1 — show understanding of the poems

- 'In a London Drawingroom' explores the speaker's attitudes towards urbanisation and industrialisation in London during the Victorian era. Similarly, 'A Wider View' also examines urbanisation and industrialisation, however, it is set in Leeds, and it switches from the Victorian era to the present-day.

AO2 — show understanding of the poets' language choices

- Both speakers reflect on the negative impact of pollution in urban areas. In 'In a London Drawingroom', the speaker describes the sky as "yellowed by smoke", which suggests the air is noxious and unclean. Similarly, in 'A Wider View', the speaker describes the "smoke-filled sky", which implies that air pollution is inescapable. Both poems suggest that human activity has damaged the environment and air pollution has made cities unpleasant and harmful to live in.

- Both poems include language associated with confinement to suggest how trapped people felt in urban areas during the Victorian period. In 'In a London Drawingroom', the speaker describes how London feels like a "huge prison-house". This suggests that overdevelopment and overcrowding has contributed to feelings of confinement, and the lack of space feels like a punishment. In 'A Wider View', the speaker describes the "panelled gates" of the factory, which suggests that the workers felt as though they were trapped by their job. Many Victorian factory workers endured long hours in dangerous conditions for little pay, however, they often couldn't leave because they wouldn't be able to survive without their wages.

- 'In a London Drawingroom' explores how the speaker feels disconnected from the people around her, which makes her feel unwelcome in London. She describes the carriages as "All closed" which suggests that she feels shut off from other Londoners. However, in 'A Wider View', the speaker's experiences of Leeds create a connection with her great-great-grandfather. She describes walking by the same buildings he would have passed, and this connection allows her to imagine meeting him "on the Wharf", suggesting that place is an important part of a person's history and identity.

AO3 — relate the poems to the context

- 'In a London Drawingroom' was written in the Victorian period during the Industrial Revolution, whereas 'A Wider View' was written in the present-day. These different time periods could account for the speakers' different perspectives of urbanisation. For Eliot, London's rapid urbanisation was happening during her lifetime, and she may have felt unhappy about the changes she was witnessing. Whereas for Seneviratne, the urbanisation of Leeds occurred before she was born, and people born in the 20th century are more accustomed to urban environments.

This answer should be marked in accordance with the levels-based mark scheme on page 134.

Make sure your answer to this question is in paragraphs and full sentences. Bullet points have been used in this example answer to suggest some information you could include.

We've included some quotes from *A Wider View* (**page 66**) in this sample answer, but direct quotes from the comparison poem aren't essential; you can use paraphrased examples or summaries to demonstrate your understanding.

ON AN AFTERNOON TRAIN FROM PURLEY TO VICTORIA, 1955 — JAMES BERRY

Caesura and end-stopping in the first stanza create a disjointed rhythm which matches the awkwardness of the strangers' initial conversation.

This suggests the speaker was surprised by the Quaker's friendliness, and he isn't used to strangers talking to him.

The poem focuses on a conversation between two strangers on a train.

Hello, she said, and startled me.
Nice day. Nice day I agreed.

This could represent the British culture of small talk about the weather.

This highlights the Quaker's ignorance. Reciting a poem to other Quakers won't do much to improve the problem of racism.

I am a Quaker she said and Sunday
I was moved in silence
5   to speak a poem loudly
for racial brotherhood.

The juxtaposition of "silence" and "loudly" suggests how strongly the Quaker felt about racial brotherhood.

This introduces the reality that some people didn't support a multicultural society.

I was thoughtful, then said
what poem came on like that?
One the moment inspired she said.
10   I was again thoughtful.

The speaker repeats "I was thoughtful", suggesting he wants to think carefully about his response.

This suggests that the Quaker's support for multi-culturalism was spur of the moment, rather than something she was passionate about.

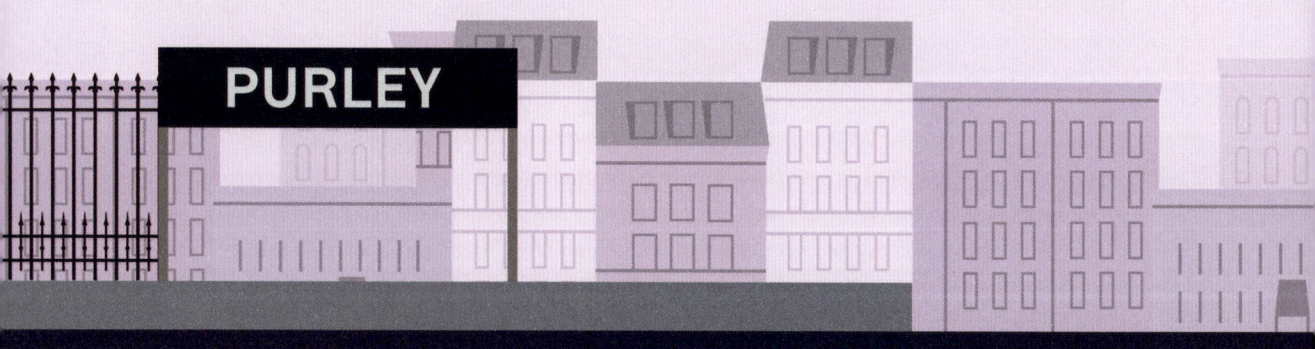

Annotation	Text	Annotation
The conversation triggers a memory.	Inexplicably I saw	
	empty city streets lit dimly	The speaker contrasts urban life in London with rural life in Jamaica.
"*darkness*" suggests Jamaica feels very far away to the speaker, suggesting he feels homesick.	in a day's first hours.	
	Alongside in darkness	
	15 was my father's big banana field.	
The line break suggests the speaker is jolted back into the present by the Quaker's question.	Where are you from? she said.	This highlights the ignorance that immigrants experience, and how they are often misunderstood.
	Jamaica I said.	
	What part of Africa is Jamaica? she said.	
This question reflects how immigrants are often questioned about their heritage.	Where Ireland is near Lapland I said.	
	20 Hard to see why you leave	The speaker replies to the Quaker's ignorance with a joke, showing his patience.
	such sunny country she said.	
"*Snow*" contrasts with "*sunny*" on the line above. This could reflect the difference in climate between Jamaica and England.	Snow falls elsewhere I said.	
	So sincere she was beautiful	The Quaker is unaware that people leave their countries out of necessity, rather than choice, highlighting her privilege.
	as people sat down around us.	
	The speaker doesn't judge the Quaker for her ignorance, and instead appreciates her sincerity.	

GCSE English Literature **Poetry Anthology** | **Worlds and Lives**

James Berry

James Berry (1924–2017) was a Jamaican-born poet, who moved to Britain in 1948, along with hundreds of others as part of the **Windrush Generation**, see below. The poem was written in 1955.

James Berry

Summary of the poem

The speaker, a Jamaican immigrant, is on a train travelling from Purley in south London to Victoria in central London. A passenger on the train speaks to him, and tells him that she is a Quaker (see **below**) and recited a poem in favour of *"racial brotherhood"*. The speaker compares life in London to the life he left behind in Jamaica. The Quaker is ignorant about Jamaica, but the speaker appreciates their conversation.

Context and references

The Windrush Generation

Following the end of World War II in 1945, the British economy had a shortage of workers. This was due to fatalities during the war, and women leaving the workforce to return to their roles as homemakers. Consequently, Britain encouraged immigration from other countries to boost the workforce. In 1948, the British Nationality Act granted British citizenship to people living in British colonies, which included those living in Jamaica. In 1948, a ship called the *Empire Windrush* transported approximately 800 migrants from Kingston, Jamaica to London. These migrants were attracted to the opportunities London could offer. Although several more ships brought migrants from the British colonies to Britain, the arrival of the *Empire Windrush* attracted significant media attention, and became the namesake of a new generation of British citizens and the start of British multiculturalism. However, many immigrants faced ignorance, prejudice and racism upon their arrival in Britain.

Passengers on the *Empire Windrush*

Comment: The poem takes place in 1955, seven years after the arrival of the *Empire Windrush*. The poem could be inspired by Berry's own experiences of immigration.

Immigrants often experience a 'culture shock' when they move to countries that are very different from their own, which can result in feelings of anxiety, uncertainty and confusion. Living in an unfamiliar environment can worsen homesickness and loneliness.

Quakers

Quakers are a Christian group. They support equality, refuse to participate in war and oppose slavery. At Quaker meetings, individuals sit in silence until someone feels moved to speak.

Comment: The Quaker speaks a poem in support of *"racial brotherhood"*. This reflects the Quaker belief in equality.

Themes

Migration

The speaker has migrated from Jamaica to London.

Belonging

The speaker reminisces about his father's "*big banana field*", suggesting that he longs for home.

Prejudice

The Quaker asks the speaker "*Where are you from?*", implying that he isn't English. This highlights the everyday racism that immigrants face, and reminds the reader that not all racism is violent or abusive; sometimes it stems from ignorance.

Form and structure

On an Afternoon Train... consists of five stanzas. Stanzas 1, 2, 3 and 5 are made up of **dialogue** between the speaker and the Quaker. The lines are written in **free verse** with **enjambment**, which reflect the natural speech patterns of a conversation.

Comment: There is very little figurative language in the poem (e.g. similes, metaphors, personification) which mirrors how people normally speak to each other.

The conversation between the two strangers is structured in a familiar way: it begins with small talk, and then becomes more personal, with each speaker revealing more about themselves.

Comment: Berry doesn't use inverted commas around the direct speech. He may have wanted to reflect how the conversation flows between the two, or to suggest the spontaneity of their conversation.

The first stanza is a typical British interaction between strangers, where the weather ("*Nice day*") is a subject for small talk.

Comment: Caesura and **end-stopping** in the first stanza creates a disjointed rhythm which reflects the initial awkwardness between the pair. The speaker is also "*startled*" by the Quaker. This could suggest that he is not used to people being friendly towards him.

The increasing stanza lengths reflect the developing conversation between the two. However, the conversation shows the miscommunication between the pair: the Quaker doesn't appear to learn anything new about migration or Jamaica. The conversation ends when more people sit near them, which implies that the Quaker's interest in the speaker is superficial and fleeting.

Comment: The conversation ending as the train gets busier could suggest that the Quaker doesn't want to be seen to be talking to an immigrant in public, hinting that she is not as open-minded as she thinks she is.

Tone

The poem has a tone of disconnection. The Quaker thinks that she has connected with the speaker, but their conversation only highlights her own ignorance, and inability to learn from him.

Language

Representation of the Quaker

Accepting

The Quaker spoke in support of "*racial brotherhood*".

Comment: The Quaker's support seems spur of the moment ("*One the moment inspired*"), hinting that her attitude may be superficial, rather than something she is truly passionate about. The Quaker is also vague about the poem she recited, which could suggest that she may not have recited a poem at all.

Self-satisfied

The Quaker is so proud of her liberal attitude she feels the need to tell the speaker.

Comment: The second stanza focuses on the Quaker's dialogue, suggesting that she takes over the conversation. The enjambment in this stanza implies she talks quickly and is eager to impress the speaker with her progressive attitude.

Ignorant

The Quaker asks why the speaker would leave a "*sunny country*". This reinforces her ignorance towards the socio-economic reasons for immigration, and highlights her own privilege. The Quaker also seems oblivious to any offence she may have caused, and she doesn't appear to learn anything from their conversation.

Comment: Although the Quaker is well-meaning, she demonstrates the ignorance that many immigrants experience.

Representation of the speaker

Polite

The speaker politely exchanges small talk with the stranger. However, he may have felt obliged to speak to the Quaker as not to seem rude.

Language continued

Representation of the speaker continued

Patient

The Quaker ignorantly thinks that Jamaica is in Africa, but the speaker responds with a joke ("*Where Ireland is near Lapland*"), rather than taking offence. He appreciates her sincerity, rather than criticising her lack of knowledge.

Comment: The speaker repeats the phrase "*I was thoughtful*" which suggests that he listens to the Quaker carefully, and considers his responses.

Homesick

The speaker pictures his "*father's big banana field*" which suggests he longs for home. The banana field is **juxtaposed** with the "*empty streets*" of London, suggesting the loneliness and isolation felt by the speaker.

Comment: The word "*father's*" hints that the speaker left his family behind when he moved to England. This reminds readers of the sacrifices that immigrants make when they move somewhere new.

Language of contrasts

The poem includes examples of contrasting language. This could hint at the disconnection between the speaker and the Quaker, as well as highlighting the differences between Jamaica and England, and the culture shock the speaker may have experienced when he immigrated.

The Quaker was "*moved in silence*" to speak "*loudly*". "*loudly*" could suggest the strength of her support for multiculturalism, but it could also hint that she enjoys hearing the sound of her own voice.

The speaker compares the "*city*" to a rural "*banana field*". This suggests that life in England is very different for the speaker.

The city streets are "*lit*" while the banana field is in "*darkness*". This could reflect how far away home seems to the speaker.

The Quaker says Jamaica is a "*sunny*" country, but the speaker refers to "*Snow*". This highlights the Quaker's ignorance: the only thing she seems to know about Jamaica is its weather.

COMPARING ON AN AFTERNOON TRAIN FROM PURLEY TO VICTORIA, 1955

Here's how *On an Afternoon Train...* could be compared to other poems.

 Remember, you can compare *On an Afternoon Train...* with any poem from the anthology as long as your response is supported with examples. The following examples suggest ways to compare the poems, but they are not complete answers.

Experiences of prejudice

The speaker in *On an Afternoon Train...* explores experiences of everyday racism. The Quaker ignorantly asks, "*What part of Africa is Jamaica?*", suggesting that she thinks all black people come from Africa. She also asks, "*Where are you from?*", implying that the speaker doesn't 'belong' in England. Despite her ignorance and insensitivity, the speaker is "*thoughtful*" when he speaks to her and appreciates her sincerity: he recognises her ignorance is not malicious. This presents him as a tolerant and patient individual, despite the prejudice he experiences as an immigrant.

Homing (**page 74**) also focuses on prejudice, specifically class prejudice surrounding regional accents in Britain. The subject of the poem takes "*hours*" of elocution lessons to hide her Midlands accent because it was associated with being working class, poor and uneducated. Because of these negative attitudes, the subject keeps her accent in "*a box beneath the bed*". This metaphor reinforces the shame she feels and the "*rusted*" lock implies that she repressed her accent for a long time. This reflects how people who experience prejudice often have to alter their identities to 'fit in'.

Longing for home

The speaker in *On an Afternoon Train...* seems to long for his home in Jamaica. He reflects on London's "*empty*" streets, which highlights the isolation and loneliness he feels living in the capital. He also recalls his "*father's big banana field*", which reminds the reader of the family the speaker may have left behind when he moved to England. However, his memory of Jamaica is shrouded in "*darkness*" which suggests that memories of his home country feel distant, hinting at the speaker's feelings of homesickness.

The speaker in *A Portable Paradise* (**page 106**) uses memories of his home country as a source of comfort and a place of refuge from the world around him. The poet, Roger Robinson, was born in London, but he spent his childhood in his family's home of Trinidad and Tobago before returning to England as a teenager. The "*paradise*" the speaker describes is reminiscent of Trinidad with "*white sands, green hills and fresh fish*", and the clear sensory language of "*piney scent*" hints that the speaker is describing a place which is meaningful to him. This suggests that people who have experienced displacement often long for their homeland.

Compare how poets present experiences of immigration in *On an Afternoon Train from Purley to Victoria, 1955* and in **one** other poem from Worlds and Lives. [30 marks]

Your answer may include:

AO1 — show understanding of the poems

- 'On an Afternoon Train...' focuses on a speaker who has immigrated from Jamaica to England, whereas 'Name Journeys' examines the experiences of a speaker who immigrated from India to Manchester. Both poems explore how immigrants can struggle to integrate into their new countries, and prejudice they may face.

AO2 — show understanding of the poets' language choices

- Both poems highlight the prejudice and ignorance experienced by immigrants. In 'On an Afternoon Train...', the Quaker asks the speaker "Where are you from?" suggesting that she thinks he is an outsider, and in 'Name Journeys', English people "stumble" when they try to pronounce the speaker's name. These examples suggest that immigrants are often made to feel like they don't belong to the countries they have relocated to.

- Both speakers experience feelings of homesickness and loneliness. In 'On an Afternoon Train...', the speaker recalls his "father's big banana field", which reminds readers how immigrants often leave their families behind. The speaker compares the banana field to London's "empty city streets", hinting at the loneliness he feels. In 'Name Journeys', the speaker also feels lonely in England, as she uses a metaphor to compare moving to Manchester as being exiled into the "wilderness" without a "companion", highlighting her feelings of isolation.

- Although both speakers experience displacement and prejudice, their tones are different. In 'On an Afternoon Train...', the speaker seems more forgiving of the people in England. He appears to appreciate the "sincere" and "beautiful" Quaker, even though she is ignorant and insensitive. However, the speaker in 'Name Journeys' is less forgiving towards British people and uses an angry tone. She criticises the "Anglo echo chamber", implying that British people do not listen to minority voices.

AO3 — relate the poems to the context

- Both poets grew up in countries which were British colonies (Berry in Jamaica and Mundair in India), and both immigrated to England. It's likely that both poems are autobiographical and explore the poets' own experiences of immigration.

This answer should be marked in accordance with the levels-based mark scheme on page 134.

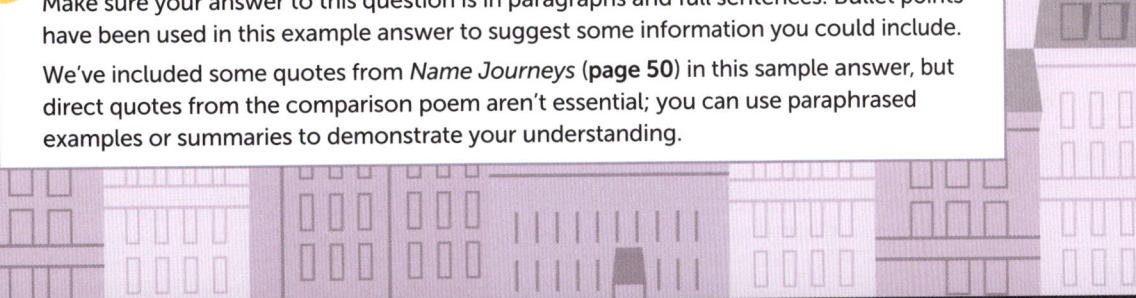

Make sure your answer to this question is in paragraphs and full sentences. Bullet points have been used in this example answer to suggest some information you could include.

We've included some quotes from *Name Journeys* (**page 50**) in this sample answer, but direct quotes from the comparison poem aren't essential; you can use paraphrased examples or summaries to demonstrate your understanding.

NAME JOURNEYS — RAMAN MUNDAIR

The speaker compares her experiences of immigration to figures from the Hindu religion. This suggests that Hinduism is important to her identity, and she finds comfort in her religion.

The poem is written in the first person, which reinforces the speaker's personal experiences.

Enjambment across stanzas emphasises this line, which hints the speaker's life has been challenging.

Unlike Rama, the speaker didn't have a "*companion*". This suggests her loneliness.

This suggests that immigrating to England was a challenging and painful experience.

This phrase highlights the connection she feels to Hinduism, and her culture.

Banyan leaves are bitter, and sugar is sweet. This reinforces the speaker's bittersweet emotions towards her experiences of immigration.

Like Rama I have felt the wilderness
but I have not been blessed

with a companion as sweet as she,
Sita; loyal, pure and true of heart.

5   Like her I have been chastened
through trial by fire. Sita and I,

spiritual sari-sisters entwined
in an infinite silk that would swathe

Draupadi's blush. My name
10 a journey between rough and smooth,

an interlacing of banyan leaves with sugar
cane. Woven tapestries of journeys;

Rama is a Hindu deity who was exiled to the "*wilderness*". Exile is a form of punishment where someone is banished from their native country. This suggests the poet views her experiences of immigration as a punishment.

"*entwined*" and "*swathe*" create an image of the speaker wrapped in silk. This suggests the speaker's heritage brings her comfort.

The contrast of "*rough and smooth*" suggests that the speaker's name, and therefore her heritage, has been both a blessing and a curse.

The speaker uses a metaphor to suggest that immigration ("*journeys*") has shaped her identity ("*Woven tapestries*").

? **chastened** — punished   **trial by fire** — 'trial by fire' was an ancient practice of setting fire to someone accused of a crime. If they were innocent, God would save them, but if they were guilty, they would burn to death. Today, it means 'to put someone under great pressure to prove their worth'.   **sari** — a traditional Indian dress   **swathe** — wrap in fabric   **banyan leaves** — bitter-tasting leaves from the banyan tree which is native to the Indian Subcontinent   **Mancunian** — from Manchester   **discordant** — unpleasant sounding   **echo chamber** — somewhere where a person only hears or sees views which agree with their own.

This line marks a turning point. The first half of the poem focuses on speaker's Indian heritage, but after she travels "*South / to North*" she concentrates on her experiences in England, highlighting how immigration caused her to feel disconnected from her Indian culture.

As the speaker grew older, she lost her mother tongue of Punjabi. The reference to "*milk teeth*" suggests the speaker was very young when she immigrated.

travelling from South

to North, where the Punjabi in my mouth

15 became dislodged as milk teeth fell

and hit infertile English soil.

"*infertile*" suggests that living in England made it difficult for her cultural identity to grow.

My mouth toiled to accommodate

the rough musicality of Mancunian vowels

"*toiled*" suggests that she struggled to learn English, and reminds the reader of the language barrier often experienced by immigrants.

Suggests that English people struggled to pronounce her name, hinting that she found integration difficult.

and my name became a stumble

20 that filled English mouths

The speaker reflects that her vibrant cultural identity has been "*dulled*" by living in England.

with a discordant rhyme, an exotic

rhythm dulled, my voice a mystery

The speaker could be criticising English people for forgetting about the colonialisation of India, or she could be suggesting that people in England expect her to forget her culture and heritage.

This suggest British people do not listen to minority voices.

in the Anglo echo chamber –

void of history and memory.

The speaker's negative experiences of immigration may evoke sympathy and encourage readers to be more welcoming to immigrants.

GCSE English Literature Poetry Anthology | Worlds and Lives

Raman Mundair

Raman Mundair is an Indian-born writer, artist and activist, who identifies as Queer. She moved to Manchester in the 1970s aged five, and currently lives in Scotland. *Name Journeys* was published in 2003.

Comment: *Name Journeys* is an **autobiographical** poem. It explores the poet's experiences of moving from India to Manchester as a child.

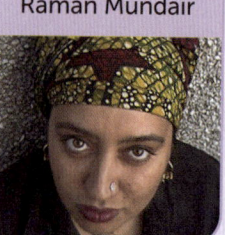

Raman Mundair

Summary of the poem

The speaker compares herself to a figure from Hinduism, Rama (see **below**), and feels an affinity with Sita, Rama's wife. She explores her experiences of immigrating from India to Manchester as a child, and the struggles she has faced living in England, such as losing her Punjabi language, and learning to speak English. The speaker reflects that immigration has shaped her identity, but she is critical of England's attitude towards ethnic minorities.

Context and references

Rama and Sita

The story of Rama and Sita appears in the *Ramayana*, an important Hindu text. Rama and Sita are a married couple who are living in exile. Sita is abducted by Ravana, an evil king, who keeps her captive. Rama wages a war against Ravana and rescues Sita. Sita is required to walk through fire to prove that she has been faithful to Rama, and she emerges from the fire unharmed.

Comment: The speaker compares her own experiences of immigration to Hindu stories. This reinforces how important her religion and Indian heritage are to her identity.

Rama and Sita

Draupadi

Draupadi appears in the Hindu text *Mahabharata*. In one story, she is brought before a group of men who try to remove her clothes. She prays to the God Krishna, who makes her sari endless so that she remains fully clothed.

Comment: The poem refers to the "*infinite silk*" that protects Draupadi's modesty.

British colonisation of India

Between 1858–1947, India was under British control. Britain benefited from this colonisation by exporting resources such as tea, pepper, silk and cotton from India at great profit. However, many Indian people lived in poverty.

Comment: The speaker criticises the "*Anglo echo chamber – / void of history and memory*". This could suggests that British people have forgotten the negative impact that colonisation had on India and its people.

Themes

Belonging

The speaker comments that English soil is *"infertile"*: she doesn't think her cultural identity can grow and flourish in England.

Spirituality & religion

The speaker feels connected to figures from her Hindu religion. She views the deity Sita as her *"spiritual sari-sister"*.

Migration

The speaker immigrated from India to Manchester as a young child.

Prejudice

The speaker criticises the *"Anglo echo chamber"*, which suggests English people don't listen to minorities.

Loneliness

The speaker describes how she hasn't been *"blessed / with a companion"*, which hints at her loneliness.

Form and structure

Name Journeys is based on a **ghazal**, a form of poetry from the Indian subcontinent that typically explores ideas around spiritual love or the pain of separation.

Comment: *Name Journeys* explores both of these ideas. It reflects the speaker's connection to her Hindu faith as well as the pain she feels being separated from her home country.

A ghazal is usually made up of **couplets** (two-line stanzas) with a set rhythm. Although *Name Journeys* consists of twelve couplets, it is written in **free verse**. The lack of rhyme or metre could reflect how the speaker feels she doesn't belong in England.

Comment: The poet may have also used a couplet structure to represent the two halves of her identity: her Indian heritage, and her life in Britain.

The poem also shares similarities with a **monologue**: it is written in the **first person**, and explores the speaker's intimate thoughts and feelings. The poem is **enjambed** throughout, so the lines flow across stanzas. This mimics the speaker's stream of consciousness and reflects the autobiographical and personal nature of the poem.

The structure of the poem reflects the speaker's relocation from India to Manchester. The first twelve lines include references to her Indian culture and heritage (see **page 54**), including her Hindu religion, saris and plants found in India (banyan leaves and sugar cane). Lines 13–14 mark a charge, when the speaker travels from *"South / to North"*, and the second half of the poem focuses on her experiences in England. This structure reinforces how she feels disconnected from her Indian heritage following her relocation. The poem ends with a criticism of British people, suggesting that they do not listen to immigrants, and they are unsympathetic towards people who suffered under British colonial rule.

Tone

The speaker is proud of her Indian heritage, and she compares her struggles to those of Hindu deities, emphasising the importance of her faith to her cultural identity.

The speaker feels dejected about her life in England. She presents it as difficult, and she struggles with feelings of isolation.

The poem ends with a critical tone, as the speaker accuses the English people of not listening to the voices of minorities, and hints that English people have forgotten the damage caused by the British colonisation of India.

Language

Language of heritage

The speaker includes references to her Indian culture, reinforcing its importance to her identity.

The speaker compares her experiences with those of Rama, Sita and Draupadi, significant figures in the Hindu religion who also overcame challenges. This suggests that she finds their stories inspiring and she is comforted by them.

The speaker refers to a sari, a traditional Indian dress. The sari is made from "*silk*", and India is one of the world's leading producers of silk.

> **Comment:** The **sibilance** in "*spiritual sari-sisters*" mimics the soft movement of silk. The speaker is also "*entwined*" in the sari, suggesting her heritage is wrapped up in her personal identity.

The speaker describes her name as an "*interlacing of banyan leaves with sugar / cane*". Banyan trees and sugar cane are native to India, so she associates her name with plants from her home country.

Language of contrast

The speaker contrasts positive and negative images throughout the poem.

- "*My name / a journey between rough and smooth*": This could suggest that she is proud that her name reflects her Indian heritage, but it has made life difficult for her in England.
- "*an interlacing of banyan leaves with sugar / cane*": Banyan leaves are bitter tasting, and the speaker contrasts this with the sweetness of sugar cane. This could reflect how her experiences of immigration have been bittersweet.
- "*a discordant rhyme, an exotic rhythm*": The speaker's name has an "*exotic rhythm*", which suggests vibrancy and excitement. However, it becomes a "*discordant rhyme*" when pronounced by English people, which suggests that living in England has made her feel disconnected from her name and therefore her identity.

Language continued

Language of difficulty

The speaker uses language from the **semantic field** of difficulty, to reflect the challenges she has faced as an immigrant.

"I have felt the wilderness"

The speaker compares immigration to being exiled into the "*wilderness*" (being banished from your homeland to somewhere remote). This suggests that she views immigration as a punishment, and the word "*wilderness*" hints at her feelings of loneliness.

"chastened / through trial by fire"

The word "*chastened*" can mean 'punished', which suggests that the speaker saw moving to England as a punishment. The phrase "*trial by fire*" suggests relocating was painful and challenging.

"dislodged as milk teeth fell"

The speaker describes how she lost her native language as she grew older. The image of milk teeth falling suggests that losing her mother tongue was an uncomfortable process.

"toiled"

This suggests that the speaker found learning English difficult, and hints at the language barrier she might have faced.

> Some immigrants don't speak the language of the country they move to. This creates a 'language barrier' where they struggle to understand and be understood, which makes it difficult to integrate into local communities.

Representation of England and English people

The speaker presents England as an unwelcoming place, which adds to the challenge of immigration, and reflects the hostility some immigrants experience from local people.

Ignorant

English people "*stumble*" when they pronounce the speaker's name. This suggests that she feels as though she doesn't belong.

Restrictive

The speaker describes "*infertile English soil*". This suggests that living in England has prevented the speaker from growing and developing her identity.

Narrow-minded

The speaker's comments about the "*Anglo echo chamber*" suggest that English people don't want to listen to the voices of immigrants.

Uncaring

English people live in a "*void of history and memory*". This hints that English people have forgotten (or do not care) about the damage caused by the British colonisation of India.

COMPARING *NAME JOURNEYS*

Here's how *Name Journeys* could be compared to other poems.

 Remember, you can compare *Name Journeys* with any poem from the anthology as long as your response is supported with examples. The following examples suggest ways to compare the poems, but they are not complete answers.

Negative experiences of immigration

Name Journeys explores the negative emotions and experiences of an immigrant. The speaker uses language associated with difficulty to describe her experiences, for example, "*chastened*", "*trial by fire*" and "*toiled*". The phrase "*trial by fire*" suggests that migration was a painful and unpleasant experience for her. The speaker reflects that moving to England has altered her in a negative way when she describes her "*exotic / rhythm dulled*". This implies that living in England has "*dulled*" her once vibrant identity.

Similarly, *pot* (**page 58**) also reflects on negative experiences of immigration. The poem focuses on a Nigerian pot that was stolen from its country and put on display in a British museum. The speaker imagines the pot returning to Nigeria, and being told "*you're not really one of us*". This highlights how immigrants struggle with feelings of belonging and acceptance when they return home. This is reinforced when the speaker describes the pot as "*empty*", which implies that leaving your home country can make an immigrant feel as though part of them is missing.

Spirituality

Name Journeys explores how religious faith can bring a person comfort. The speaker likens her experiences of immigration to those of Rama, a deity from the Hindu religion who was exiled to a "*wilderness*". Comparing herself to Rama suggests that she identifies with the difficulties he experienced, and that the speaker's religious faith brought her comfort and helped her overcome the challenges she faced as an immigrant.

Shall earth no more inspire thee (**page 26**) considers how a spiritual connection to nature can bring someone comfort. The speaker describes how the subject's "*spirit*" bends in "*fond idolatry*" when they watch a sunset. This likens being in nature to a religious experience, and the word "*fond*" suggest that this brings the subject comfort. The speaker in the poem could be interpreted as God, as they say "*nought beside can bless thee*", suggesting that only God can comfort the subject through his control of the natural world.

Compare how poets present ideas about identity in *Name Journeys* and in **one** other poem from Worlds and Lives. [30 marks]

Your answer may include:

AO1 — show understanding of the poems

- Both 'Name Journeys' and 'Homing' explore the importance of language on someone's identity. Both speakers reflect how their accent and language have caused difficulties and challenges, especially in relation to connecting with their local community. However, both speakers are proud of the culture that their language represents.

AO2 — show understanding of the poets' language choices

- Both speakers explore what it is like to lose their accent and language. In 'Name Journeys', the speaker describes how the "Punjabi in my mouth / became dislodged" when she moved from India to England. The word "dislodged" suggests that she was forced to lose her native language against her will. In 'Homing', the speaker describes elocution lessons, with the "teacher's ruler across your legs". This implies that the subject was also forced to lose their regional accent through corporal punishment.

- Both speakers reflect on the challenges that their accent and language have caused. In 'Name Journeys' the speaker "toiled" to learn English. The word "toiled" suggests that learning English as a second language was difficult for her. In 'Homing', the subject keeps her accent in a "box beneath the bed". This metaphor suggests that the subject felt ashamed of her accent, and needed to keep it hidden.

- Both speakers feel pride towards their accent and language. In 'Name Journeys', the speaker compares her name to "banyan leaves with sugar / cane". These items both grow in India, which suggests her Indian heritage is entwined with her name and an important part of her identity. Similarly, in 'Homing', the speaker wants to "lick the coal" from the sounds of the Midlands accent. The Midlands has a proud mining heritage, so this metaphor suggests that the speaker celebrates her local identity.

AO3 — relate the poems to the context

- Both poems are autobiographical accounts of the poets' experiences of language and identity, so the thoughts and feelings expressed in the poems are authentic. Mundair moved from India to England when she was a child, and Berry was born and raised in the Midlands.

This answer should be marked in accordance with the levels-based mark scheme on page 134.

⭐ Make sure your answer to this question is in paragraphs and full sentences. Bullet points have been used in this example answer to suggest some information you could include.

We've included some quotes from *Homing* (**page 74**) in this sample answer, but direct quotes from the comparison poem aren't essential; you can use paraphrased examples or summaries to demonstrate your understanding.

POT — SHAMSHAD KHAN

These phrases introduce excuses given by governments and museums why they cannot return stolen artefacts to their native countries.

"*they*" could refer to governments and museums.

so big — they said you shouldn't really be moved

so fragile you might break

you could be from anywhere pot

styles have travelled just like terracotta

5 you could almost be an english pot

but I know you're not.

The speaker addresses the pot directly, suggesting it is a living thing. The pot could symbolise communities affected by colonialism.

This suggests how difficult it can be for immigrants to integrate into a new country.

I know half of the story pot
of where you come from
of how you got here

The pot is silent throughout. This reflects how immigrants are often voiceless because they have little power in society.

10 but I need you to tell me the rest pot

tell me

"*they*" creates a sense of opposition between the speaker and the people who took the pot.

did they say you were bought pot
a looters' deal done
the whole lot

This suggests museums are often vague and untruthful about how they acquire foreign objects.

15 sold to the gentleman in the grey hat

or

did they say you were lost pot

finders are keepers you know pot

"*looters*" implies that the pot was stolen.

The stereotypical image of a British man was a 'gentleman in a hat'. This description hints that the man responsible for taking the pot was British.

or

This childish phrase creates a sarcastic tone which reinforces the speaker's disdain towards the people who took the pot.

20 did they say they didn't notice you pot
must have slipped onto the white sailing yacht

bound for england.
someone
somewhere

The word "*white*" hints that white Europeans took the pot. Yachts are also associated with wealth, suggesting that the pot was taken by someone rich and powerful.

25 will have missed you pot
gone out looking for you pot
because

This reminds the reader of the impact of colonialism and the feelings of loss felt by those who had people and objects taken from them.

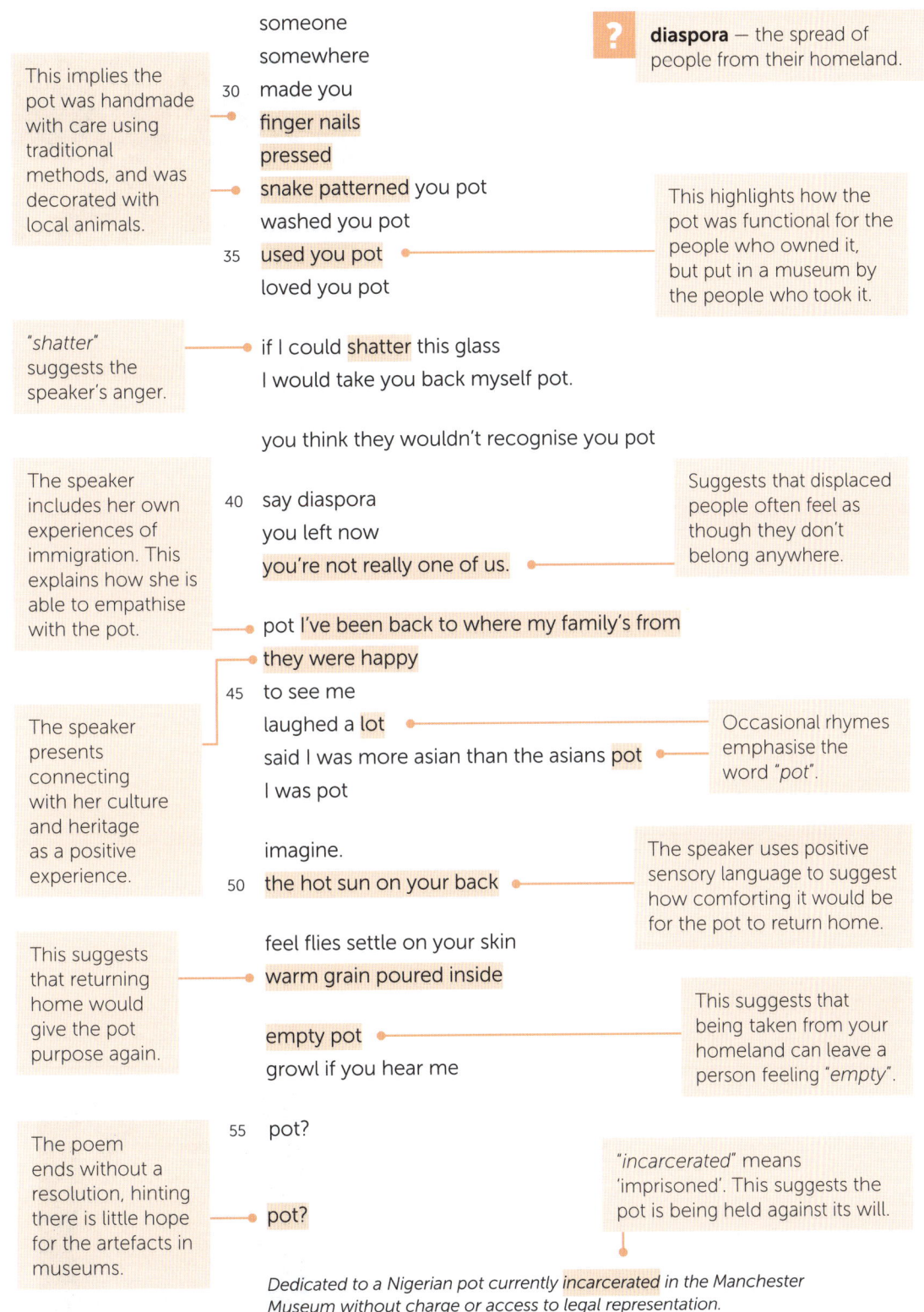

Shamshad Khan

Shamshad Khan was born in England 1964. Her parents are of Pakistani heritage. *pot* was published in her 2007 collection *Megalomaniac*.

Shamshad Khan

Comment: The speaker is likely to be Khan herself, and she could be projecting her own experiences of being a first-generation immigrant on to the pot in the poem.

Summary of the poem

The speaker addresses a Nigerian pot on display in the Manchester Museum. The speaker asks the pot how it was taken from its homeland, who made it and whether its owners would recognise it if it was returned. The speaker reflects on her own positive experiences of returning to her family's homeland, and imagines how the pot would feel if it returned to Nigeria.

Comment: The poem was commissioned by the Manchester Museum.

Context and references

European colonisation

From around the 16th century, powerful European countries such as Spain, England and France began travelling abroad to the Americas, Asia and Africa. Often, these European countries claimed land overseas, irrespective of the people who had lived there for centuries. As well as claiming land, colonisers would often enslave local people, pillage their resources and take items of value. Many of these colonies existed up until the 20th century, and some still exist today.

Comment: Pakistan, where Khan's parents are from, was a British colony until 1947, and Nigeria (where the pot is from) was a British colony until 1960.

Museum artefacts

This poem is about a pot from Nigeria which was on display in the Manchester Museum. There is a lot of controversy around museum artefacts which have been acquired from overseas. Often these artefacts were taken without permission, and many people believe they should be returned.

A Nigerian pot, similar to the one from the poem.

Comment: Some museums refuse to return items because they claim the items are too large or fragile to be safely returned. The speaker highlights these excuses in the poem's opening lines.

Themes

Migration
The pot has been taken from its owners in Nigeria. The speaker reflects on her experiences returning to her family's homeland

Identity
The speaker suggests that immigrants can struggle with their identity. She comments that the pot "*could be from anywhere*".

Belonging
The speaker imagines the pot returning to Nigeria and being told it is no longer "*one of us*". This highlights how immigrants often feel as though they don't belong in either their 'new' country or their 'old' country.

Form and structure

The poem is largely written in **free verse** with frequent **enjambment**, which more closely resembles the patterns of natural speech. This reflects the conversational style of the poem, and the speaker's desire to create a close bond with the pot.

Occasionally, the speaker emphasises the word "*pot*" by rhyming it with "*not*", "*lot*" and "*yacht*".

Comment: The speaker doesn't use capital letters or conventional punctuation. This reinforces the conversational style, but also hints that the speaker isn't afraid to challenge what people agree is 'correct'.

The speaker addresses the pot with **rhetorical questions**, but the pot doesn't reply. This could reflect how immigrants and colonised people are often voiceless. The pot's silence also reflects how the issue of returning foreign artefacts to their country of origin remains unresolved.

Tone

The speaker has an ironic tone. She imagines the excuses the museum will give for not returning the pot to Nigeria, and the lies told by the people who took the pot from its homeland.

The speaker also uses an empathetic tone. She tries to connect with the pot, and imagines how it longs to be reunited with its owners in Nigeria.

Comment: The speaker uses imperative verbs such as "*tell*", "*imagine*", "*feel*" and "*growl*" to encourage the pot to acknowledge the struggles it has faced and to reflect on its identity.

The speaker is angry towards the people who took the pot and the museum that refuses to send it home. She wants to "*shatter*" the glass around the exhibit and "*take [it] back*" to Nigeria.

Language

Representation of the pot

Although the poem focuses on a pot, the poem can be interpreted as an **allegory** for people who have experienced displacement or have been colonised by other countries.

> **Comment:** The pot is displayed in a museum for people to look at. This could reflect how immigrants often feel they are being judged and scrutinised by local people.

The speaker **anthropomorphises** the pot (gives it human characteristics).

- She addresses the pot as if it were a living thing, using the second-person pronoun "*you*".
- She asks the pot questions, and expects it to respond: "*growl if you hear me / pot?*"
- She imagines the pot can feel human sensations, such as "*flies settle on [its] skin*".

Presenting the pot as a living thing allows the speaker to connect with it, and reflect on the emotions felt by immigrants.

> **Comment:** The pot stays silent which could reflect how immigrants are often voiceless.

Representation of belonging and displacement

The speaker explores how displaced people struggle with feelings of belonging. The speaker imagines the pot returning to Nigeria, and the owners rejecting it: "*you're not really one of us*". This reflects how some immigrants feel as though they don't belong to either their homeland or the country where they have settled.

> **Comment:** The speaker's own experiences of returning to her homeland are presented positively. Her family were "*happy*" to see her and they "*laughed a lot*". This emphasises the importance of staying connected with your culture and identity.

The speaker imagines the negative consequences of the pot being taken from its home:

 The pot is missed by its owners who have "*gone out looking*" for it. This suggests that displacement can tear families apart.

 The pot "*could almost be… english*", which reinforces how immigrants can struggle with their identity.

 The pot is denied "*the hot sun on [its] back*". This suggests that immigrants can lose their connection to their homeland.

 The pot doesn't have a purpose in the museum: it is "*empty*", rather than full of "*warm grain*". This could reflect how some immigrants feel unfulfilled.

Language continued

Representation of the colonisers

The speaker implies that white Europeans were responsible for taking the pot:

- The image of the *"gentleman in the grey hat"* represents the stereotypical British 'gentleman'.
- The *"yacht"* is *"white"*, which could allude to the skin colour of the people who took the pot. Yachts are often associated with wealth, so this reminds the reader of the power the white people had over the people they colonised.
- The boat was *"bound for England"*.

A stereotypical British gentleman.

The poem suggests the pot had no choice when it was taken. This could reflect how countries were often forced to accept colonisation.

> **Comment:** The speaker wants to separate herself from the colonisers, and uses the third person plural *"they"* (rather than 'we') to create distance.

The speaker presents the colonisers negatively.

Thieves

The speaker refers to the person who took the pot as a *"looter"*, implying that they stole the pot.

Liars

The speaker suggests several reasons why the pot was taken from Nigeria: it was *"bought"*, it was *"lost"* and it *"slipped"* on to a boat. It's implied that these are all lies to hide the fact it was stolen.

> **Comment:** The looter's 'innocent' reasons for having the pot suggests he knew he'd done something wrong by taking it, and needed to lie to cover up his crime.

Representation of the museum

The speaker also blames the museum for keeping the pot separated from its home.

- The museum claims the pot is *"too big"* and *"too fragile"* to be returned safely. The speaker implies these are just excuses to keep the pot in the museum.
- The speaker describes the pot as *"incarcerated in the Manchester Museum without charge"*. This suggests that the pot has been wrongfully imprisoned and held against its will.
- The speaker claims the pot doesn't have *"legal representation"*. This could reflect how some immigrants struggle to access services due to language barriers, lack of money or unfamiliarity with the system.

COMPARING *POT*

Here's how *pot* could be compared to other poems.

 Remember, you can compare *pot* with any poem from the anthology as long as your response is supported with examples. The following examples suggest ways to compare the poems, but they are not complete answers.

Belonging

pot explores ideas around belonging, and how individuals who relocate from one country to another often feel as though they don't belong to either their 'old' or 'new' countries. In the poem, the speaker tells the pot "*you could almost be an english pot / but I know you're not*". This reflects how some immigrants struggle to integrate into their new country, and how they feel as though they don't belong. Similarly, the speaker also says that the pot's owners in Nigeria "*wouldn't recognise*" it, reinforcing how some immigrants are also rejected by the communities they leave behind. This highlights how displacement can lead to feelings of isolation and loneliness.

These themes are also explored in *On an Afternoon Train...* (**page 42**). The Quaker asks the speaker "*Where are you from?*", implying that his black skin makes him an 'outsider'. Although the Quaker probably didn't mean to cause offence, the insensitivity of her question may have reminded the speaker that he doesn't 'belong' to English society.

Cultural pride

The speaker in *pot* reflects on her own positive experiences of reconnecting with her culture. She visits where her "*family's from*" and describes how "*happy*" they were and how they "*laughed a lot*". This suggests that reconnecting with your heritage can be a joyful experience. The speaker comments that she was "*more asian than the asians*", which suggests the pride she has for her Asian culture, and the importance that this has on her identity.

The speaker in *Homing* (**page 74**) explores the pride she feels towards the Midlands accent, and its association with heavy industry. The speaker wanted a Midlands accent she could "*shout... from the roofs*", suggesting the pride and admiration she feels towards it. She describes the vowels in the accent as being "*ferrous as nails*", and this simile links the Midlands accent to the area's history of iron production.

64 ClearRevise

Compare how poets present ideas about oppression in *pot* and in **one** other poem from Worlds and Lives. [30 marks]

Your answer may include:

AO1 — show understanding of the poems
- Both 'pot' and 'England in 1819' explore ideas about oppression and control. 'pot' focuses on a pot which was taken from Nigeria and displayed in the Manchester Museum. The speaker is angry that the pot was stolen, and that the museum refuses to return it. 'pot' could be interpreted as an allegory for colonialism, and how colonies were oppressed by European countries. In 'England in 1819', the speaker is angry that powerful institutions, such as the monarchy and the government, oppress English people and cause them to suffer.

AO2 — show understanding of the poets' language choices
- Both poems have an angry tone. In 'pot, the speaker threatens to "shatter" the glass cabinet the pot is kept in. The word "shatter" suggests she wants to forcibly break it, which implies her rage towards the colonial oppressors who stole the pot. In 'England in 1819', the speaker uses caesura to create a choppy, disjointed rhythm. This suggests that the speaker is overwhelmed by the anger he feels towards the powerful institutions that oppress ordinary people.
- Both speakers explore the unhappiness of those who have been oppressed. In 'pot', the speaker describes the pot as "empty", which suggests it is unfulfilled while it remains in the museum, and that it has lost its sense of purpose. In 'England in 1819', the speaker describes the English public as being "starved and stabbed" by their oppressors, which suggests that they are miserable and afraid.
- Both speakers represent the oppressors negatively. In 'pot', the people who stole the pot are referred to using the third person pronoun "they". This creates a division between the speaker and the pot, and the people who took it. The men who took the pot are presented as "looters", who lied about how they came to own the pot. This highlights how powerful people abuse their power to benefit themselves. In 'England in 1819', the speaker also uses the third person pronoun "they" to acknowledge a division between the ruling classes and the English public. The speaker compares the monarchy to leeches. This suggests that the king is a parasite who feeds off the country's strength.

AO3 — relate the poems to the context
- Although both poems explore different forms of oppression (colonialism in 'pot', and abuse of power in 'England in 1819'), both poets hoped to encourage change. In 'pot', Khan hopes that the Manchester Museum and British government will agree to return the pot to Nigeria, whereas in 'England in 1819' Shelley may have hoped that the English public would have rebelled against the monarchy, inspired by the events of the French Revolution.

This answer should be marked in accordance with the levels-based mark scheme on page 134.

Make sure your answer to this question is in paragraphs and full sentences. Bullet points have been used in this example answer to suggest some information you could include.

We've included some quotes from *England in 1819* (**page 18**) in this sample answer, but direct quotes from the comparison poem aren't essential; you can use paraphrased examples or summaries to demonstrate your understanding.

A WIDER VIEW — SENI SENEVIRATNE

From the backyard of his back-to-back,
my great-great-grandad searched for spaces
in the smoke-filled sky to stack his dreams,
high enough above the cholera to keep them
5   and his newborn safe from harm.

In eighteen sixty-nine, eyes dry with dust
from twelve hours combing flax beneath
the conicals of light in Marshall's Temple Mill,
he took the long way home because
10 he craved the comfort of a wider view.

As he passed the panelled gates of Tower Works,
the tall octagonal crown of Harding's chimney
drew his sights beyond the limits of his working life
drowned the din of engines, looms and shuttles
15 with imagined peals of ringing bells.

Today, my footsteps echo in the sodium gloom
of Neville Street's Dark Arches and the red-brick vaults
begin to moan as time, collapsing in the River Aire,
sweeps me out to meet him on the Wharf.

20 We stand now, timeless in the flux of time, anchored
only by the axis of our gaze – a ventilation shaft
with gilded tiles, and Giotto's geometric lines –
while the curve of past and future generations
arcs between us.

Annotations:

- The repetition of "*back*" reinforces the sense of confinement.
- The speaker imagines the unpleasant conditions her great-great-grandad experienced in 19th century Leeds: cramped housing, a "*smoke-filled sky*" and the threat of disease.
- Although he is tired from his shift, he walks "*the long way home*", suggesting he wanted time to himself.
- Alliteration emphasises his discomfort.
- The speaker references real places in Leeds.
- This adds to the feeling of confinement.
- The buildings seem imposing, and "*crown*" suggests the power of the factory owners over their workers.
- This suggests he dreams of a better life.
- The triplet emphasises the noise of the factory
- The poem shifts to the present and a first-person perspective.
- Personification creates a supernatural tone,
- The plural pronoun "*We*" emphasises the speaker's connection with her relative.
- The buildings in Leeds create a sense of physical belonging for the speaker and make her feel connected to her great-great-grandfather.

? **cholera** — a deadly disease spread through unclean water   **flax** — a plant used to make a cloth called linen   **octagonal** — having eight sides   **din** — noise   **loom** — a frame used for weaving fabric   **shuttle** — a tool used in fabric production   **sodium** — a substance used in street lights   **Wharf** — a place on the edge of a waterway where ships can load and unload cargo   **flux** — change   **axis** — a point around which something revolves

Seni Seneviratne

Seni Seneviratne

Seni Seneviratne is a creative artist who was born and raised in Leeds. Her grandfather was from Sri Lanka, and moved to Leeds in 1928. *A Wider View* was written in 2007.

Comment: The poem refers to real places in Leeds (see **below**) which adds to its authenticity.

Summary of the poem

The speaker imagines what life was like for her great-great-grandfather in 19th century Leeds and the difficulties he faced: cramped housing, pollution, disease, and working long hours in a factory. She imagines him walking around the streets of Leeds dreaming of a better life. The poem shifts to the present, and the speaker looks at the same buildings her ancestor would have walked past. Sharing this experience makes her feel connected to her great-great-grandfather, despite living centuries apart.

Context and references

19th century Leeds

Leeds, a city in Northern England, was an important place for flax manufacturing during the Industrial Revolution (see **pages 11** and **35**). Factories spun flax into linen, a textile used in clothes.

People moved from the countryside to work in the factories. This led to overcrowding which caused health and social problems.

Comment: The speaker's great-great-grandfather lived in a "*back-to-back*": a house built very close to others. He also worries about "*cholera*", a disease that easily spread in overcrowded areas.

Work in the factories was hard and unpleasant, and many working-class families struggled to make ends meet. Unlike today, there was little protection for workers and many wouldn't dare to complain about the conditions because they depended on the income their job provided.

Comment: The great-great-grandfather's eyes are "*dry with dust*" and he works "*twelve hour*" days.

The poem references several real places in Leeds that were associated with linen production.

- **Marshall's Temple Mill**: A mill which spun flax into linen and was one of the largest factories in the world.
- **Tower Works**: A factory which made steel pins for use in the textile industry.
- **Dark Arches**: A network of brick arches beneath Leeds railway station.
- **Harding's Chimney**: Three distinctive chimneys which were part of the Tower Works. One of the chimneys was based on a tower designed by Giotto, an Italian architect.

Comment: The poem refers to "*Giotto's geometric lines*".

Marshall's Temple Mill, 1855

Themes

Environmental damage
The factories have created a *"smoke-filled sky"*.

Belonging
The Victorian buildings allow the speaker to feel connected to her distant relative, as well as other *"generations"* of her family.

Form and structure

The poem is made up of five stanzas, and each stanza consists of one sentence. The lines are written in **free verse**, and are **enjambed**. This helps the narrative to flow, and creates a strong sense of the speaker's voice and reinforces her reflective tone.

The first three stanzas are written in the **third person**, and the speaker imagines her great-great-grandfather's life in 19th century Leeds and the difficulties he faced.

> **Comment:** Reflecting on her great-great-grandfather's life reinforces the importance of family heritage to the speaker's identity.

The fourth stanza jumps to the present day and switches to the **first person** as the speaker walks around Leeds. Structuring the poem in this way highlights how the buildings in Leeds allow the speaker to feel connected to her great-great-grandfather.

> **Comment:** In the final stanza, the speaker uses the plural pronouns *"We"* and *"us"* to emphasise the connection she feels with her great-great-grandfather.

Tone

The poem has a thoughtful tone as the speaker imagines what life would have been like for her ancestor, and acknowledges the difficulties he faced.

The poem also focuses on feelings of connection, and how the city of Leeds connects *"past and future generations"* of the speaker's family.

Language

Representation of 19th century Leeds

The speaker uses **sensory language** to describe how industrialisation negatively affected her great-great-grandfather's life in 19th century Leeds.

He sees a *"smoke-filled sky"*, suggesting the pollution caused by the factories. He also sees the *"tall octagonal crown"* of the factory's chimney. The *"tall"* chimney suggests it is imposing, and its *"crown"* could represent the factory owners' power and control over the people in Leeds.

Working in the factory make his eyes *"dry with dust"*. The **alliteration** in this phrase emphasises his feelings of discomfort.

He hears *"engines, looms and shuttles"*. The **triplet** reinforces the noise of the factory.

Comment: He *"drowned the din"* of the factory with the imaginary sound of *"bells"*. This could represent his longing for freedom.

Most working-class Victorians didn't work on Sundays so that they could attend church. Church bells would typically ring on Sundays to call people to worship, so the speaker's great-great-grandfather may have associated church bells with freedom from work.

Representation of the speaker's great-great-grandfather

Troubled

He is concerned about his family dying from cholera, especially his *"newborn"*.

Hard-working

He works *"twelve hours"* a day in the factory

Hopeful

He *"searched for spaces / ... to stack his dreams"*, which suggests that he actively looked for ways to build a better life for himself and his family. He also *"craved a wider view"*, and the verb *"craved"* reinforces how desperate he was to escape his difficult life.

Comment: The speaker creates sympathy for her great-great-grandfather by acknowledging the struggles he faced. Without his determination to survive, the speaker's *"past and future generations"* may not have existed. This reinforces the importance of family on a person's heritage.

Language continued

Language of confinement

The speaker uses language associated with confinement to reinforce how her great-great-grandfather was trapped by poverty.

Comment: In the 19th century, working-class people were often trapped in a cycle of poverty. People were forced to work in terrible conditions for very low wages. However, many people stayed in these jobs because they depended on them for survival.

 The phrase "*backyard of his back-to-back*" suggests that working-class housing in the 19th century was cramped. The repetition of "*back*" also suggests that many people were pushed back by people with money and power.

 The phrase "*searched for spaces*" implies that there was little room in the city, and the **sibilance** suggests that lots of people were squeezed into a small space.

 The "*panelled gates*" of the factory suggests that workers were confined inside, but also how the threat of poverty means they cannot leave their dangerous jobs.

Language continued

Supernatural elements

When the poem jumps to the present in the fourth stanza, the speaker introduces several supernatural elements. This suggests that looking at the Victorian buildings in Leeds creates a strong connection between the speaker and her great-great-grandfather, which almost makes her feel as though she can travel through time to meet him. This reinforces the importance of place and family to a person's identity.

- She describes how the *"red-brick vaults / begin to moan"*, and this eerie personification signals a shift towards the supernatural.
- The speaker describes *"time, collapsing"* which is a powerful, supernatural image. It suggests that walking the same streets as her great-great-grandfather creates a connection between them, which allows her to feel close to him, despite living centuries apart.
- The phrase *"sweeps me out to meet him"* suggests that the speaker is able to time travel, and the assonance of the long 'e' sound in *"sweeps"*, *"me"* and *"meet"* helps to emphasise the fluidity of her movement through time.
- The final stanza appears to take place outside the confines of time, as she stands beside her great-great-grandfather.
- The speaker describes how *"the curve of past and future generations / arcs"* between her and her great-great-grandfather as they look at the same *"ventilation shaft"*. This ghostly image reinforces how place can connect us to our ancestors.

Comment: The supernatural elements suggest that the speaker's connection to her great-great-grandfather is more powerful than time.

COMPARING *A WIDER VIEW*

Here's how *A Wider View* could be compared to other poems.

 Remember, you can compare *A Wider View* with any poem from the anthology as long as your response is supported with examples. The following examples suggest ways to compare the poems, but they are not complete answers.

Oppression

A Wider View presents a clear impression of life in Victorian Leeds for the working class. The speaker describes the cramped housing ("*back-to-back*"), threat of disease ("*cholera*") and long working hours ("*twelve hours combing flax*"). This suggests that working-class people were oppressed by the wealthy who wanted to keep the working classes poor, so that they could be exploited for profit. In *A Wider View*, the "*tall*" factory chimneys with a "*crown*" hint at the power of the factory owners who oppress working-class people like the speaker's great-great-grandfather.

England in 1819 (see **page 18**) also examines how ordinary English people were oppressed by powerful institutions in the 19th century. The speaker personifies England as "*fainting*" because the "*leechlike*" rulers have abused their power and exploited the public. This oppression is reinforced when the speaker describes English people as being "*starved and stabbed*", suggesting that powerful institutions oppress people using violence and hunger.

Belonging

In *A Wider View*, the speaker feels connected to her great-great-grandfather as she looks at the Victorian buildings in Leeds that he would have walked past. She uses the plural pronouns "*We*" and "*us*" to reinforce the connection she feels with her great-great-grandfather and their shared experiences. This suggests that Leeds evokes a powerful sense of family history and belonging for the speaker, and she feels connected to the city because of her family's past.

In *A Portable Paradise* (see **page 106**), the speaker also explores his connection to a place, and its association with his grandmother. The speaker comments, "*if I speak of Paradise, then I am speaking of my grandmother*" which emphasises the connection between the two, and the importance of family for feelings of belonging.

Compare how poets present ideas about identity in *A Wider View* and in **one** other poem from Worlds and Lives. [30 marks]

Your answer may include:

AO1 — show understanding of the poems

- Both 'A Wider View' and 'The Jewellery Maker' explore how family, work and place all affect a person's identity. In 'A Wider View', the speaker imagines her great-great-grandfather's experiences working in a factory in Victorian Leeds. 'The Jewellery Maker' examines the daily life of a goldsmith.

AO2 — show understanding of the poets' language choices

- Both the great-great-grandfather and the jewellery maker's identities are shaped by their work. In 'A Wider View', the speaker describes her great-great-grandfather as working "twelve hours" a day "combing flax" in a factory. This presents him as hard-working. In 'The Jewellery Maker', the goldsmith isn't given a name and is only referred to as "The Jewellery Maker" emphasising how important his occupation is to his identity.

- Both speakers suggest that family is an important part of a person's identity. In 'A Wider View', the speaker uses the plural pronouns "We" and "us" to describe how her perceptions of Leeds are intertwined with those of her great-great-grandfather. Even though they have never met, the speaker acknowledges their shared experiences which brings them closer together. In 'The Jewellery Maker', the goldsmith's craft has been passed down through generations: "like his father before him, and his father too". This suggests that making jewellery is an important part of his family's history.

- Both speakers suggest that place also contributes to a person's identity. In 'A Wider View', the speaker includes multiple references to historical buildings in Leeds, such as "Marshall's Temple Mill" and "Neville Street's Dark Arches", to emphasise the importance of Leeds to both the speaker's identity, as well as her great-great-grandfather's. In 'The Jewellery Maker', the speaker use sensory language to create a clear sense of place, for example the "smell of blossom", the sound of a "wild dog" and the feel of "heat-baked stone". This creates a sense of familiarity and emphasises how the jewellery belongs to his community.

AO3 — relate the poems to the context

- It is likely that both speakers are drawing on their own identities in their poems. Seneviratne was born and raised in Leeds, so her descriptions of Leeds reflect her experiences. Although the setting of 'The Jewellery Maker' is never clearly stated, it could be based in Ghana. Adjoa Parker is of Ghanaian descent, and Ghana was known as Gold Coast because of its gold mines, so it's possible that Adjoa Parker was inspired by her cultural heritage.

This answer should be marked in accordance with the levels-based mark scheme on page 134.

Make sure your answer to this question is in paragraphs and full sentences. Bullet points have been used in this example answer to suggest some information you could include.

We've included some quotes from *The Jewellery Maker* (**page 90**) in this sample answer, but direct quotes from the comparison poem aren't essential; you can use paraphrased examples or summaries to demonstrate your understanding.

HOMING — LIZ BERRY

"rusted" suggests the subject repressed their accent for a long time.

A phrase used in elocution lessons.

"escape" associates a regional accent with freedom.

This suggests that the subject may have passed away.

Regional dialect words add to the authenticity of the poem.

Anaphora of *"I wanted"* reinforces how the speaker longs for the person's accent to feel as though she belongs to the Midlands.

The speaker would be proud of a Midlands accent.

"pigeons" links to the title *Homing* (see **page 76**).

For years you kept your accent
in a box beneath the bed,
the lock rusted shut by hours of elocution
how now brown cow
5   the teacher's ruler across your legs.

We heard it escape sometimes,
a guttural *uh* on the phone to your sister,
saft or *blart* to a taxi driver
unpacking your bags from his boot.
10 I loved its thick drawl, g's that rang.

Clearing your house, the only thing
I wanted was that box, jemmied open
to let years of lost words spill out —
bibble, fittle, tay, wum,
15 vowels ferrous as nails, consonants

you could lick the coal from.
I wanted to swallow them all: the pits,
railways, factories thunking and clanging
the night shift, the red brick
20 back-to-back you were born in.

I wanted to forge your voice
in my mouth, a blacksmith's furnace;
shout it from the roofs,
send your words, like pigeons,
25 fluttering for home.

The speaker uses the second person to address an unknown subject.

This suggests that the elocution lessons were strict: speaking incorrectly could result in physical punishment.

This suggests that the accent slipped out around other local people.

Consonance emphasises the sounds in the accent.

"jemmied" suggests that the box was firmly shut but that the speaker was desperate to open it.

These images link the Midlands accent with its heritage of coal mining and iron production.

Onomatopoeia helps the reader imagine the sounds of factories.

"forge" and *"blacksmith's furnace"* link the accent to iron production.

Ending the poem with *"home"* reinforces the importance of place to a person's identity.

? **elocution** — the study of speaking the 'accepted' form of a language, often to sound better educated   **guttural** — a sound made in the throat   **saft** — silly   **blart** — cry
jemmied — forced open with a crowbar   **bibble** — pebble   **fittle** — food   **tay** — tea
wum — home   **ferrous** — containing iron

Liz Berry

Liz Berry (b. 1980) is a poet from the Midlands, an area in the centre of England. *Homing* was published in 2014 in a collection called *Black Country,* which is a name for an area in the Midlands (see **page 76**).

Liz Berry

Summary of the poem

The speaker addresses an unknown subject, possibly a family member, and recalls how they disguised their Midlands accent following strict elocution lessons. The speaker remembers how the person's accent would slip out occasionally when speaking to family members or other local people. The speaker wishes they could speak with the person's accent and dialect because it reminds them of their heritage and home.

Context and references

Received Pronunciation

During the second half of the 20th century, television, cinema and radio grew in popularity. Most actors and broadcasters spoke with an accent known as **Received Pronunciation** (RP): a formal-sounding accent that many considered the 'correct' way to speak. RP was associated with being well educated, wealthy and successful, whereas people with regional accents were often considered uneducated, poor and working class.

A family watching the TV in 1950s

Comment: The speaker hints that the poem is addressed to someone with a working-class background. They grew up in a *"back-to-back"* (houses which share three walls with adjoining houses, which were built cheaply for local workers).

Some people with regional accents aspired to have an RP accent, so would attend elocution lessons to learn how to speak with an RP accent.

Comment: The poem includes the phrase *"how now brown cow"* which was used in elocution lessons to practise the 'ow' vowel sound.

Nowadays, regional accents are heard much more widely on TV and radio, and they are a source of pride for many people.

Context continued

Regional accents

England has lots of regional accents, and you can often tell where a person is from by the way they pronounce words, or the language they use. **Dialect words** are words used by regional communities which may not be understood by people outside of that community.

Comment: The poem includes the dialect words "*bibble, fettle, tay, wum*" which may not be recognisable to anyone outside the Midlands.

The Black Country

The Black Country is the name given to an area of the Midlands west of Birmingham, including places such as Dudley, Sandwell, Walsall and Wolverhampton. The area became one of the most industrial parts of Britain, thanks to its coal mines and iron production. The area got its name from the soot that covered the region from factories.

A young miner in the Black Country, c1920s

Comment: The speaker describes "*consonants / you could lick the coal from*" linking the Midlands accent to its role in coal mining.

Homing pigeons

Homing pigeons are a species of bird which have been selectively bred for their ability to find their way home over long distances of up to 1,000 miles. Before telephones were invented, people used pigeons to send messages over long distances.

Comment: The title of the poem, *Homing*, and the line "*send your words like pigeons*" both refer to homing pigeons. This could represent how the speaker never forgets her identity, even when she is far from home. Birds often represent freedom, so the **simile** could reflect how changing attitudes towards regional accents have freed the speaker from feeling shame about the way she speaks.

Themes

Identity

The speaker links their identity with the Midlands accent and its industrial heritage.

Prejudice

The speaker addresses someone who was forced to take "*hours of elocution*" lessons because their Midlands accent was seen as 'inferior'. This reminds the reader of the prejudice towards regional accents which existed in England.

Belonging

The speaker longs for a Midlands accent as a sign that she belongs to the area.

Form and structure

Homing consists of five stanzas, each with five lines. The poem directly addresses an unknown subject using the second-person pronoun "*you*".

Comment: The speaker's memories of the subject are in the **past tense**, and the speaker describes "*Clearing*" the subject's house. This could suggest that the poem is addressed to a relative or friend who has passed away. It is likely that the subject is older than the speaker as they experienced prejudice towards their accent which has now largely disappeared.

The poem is written in **free verse** and uses **enjambment**. This more closely resembles natural speech, and adds to the conversational style of the poem, hinting at the closeness between the speaker and the person they are addressing.

The first two stanzas describe how the subject was made to feel that their Midlands accent was 'inferior', so they took elocution lessons to disguise it. Stanzas 3-5 focus on the speaker's desire to have a Midlands accent, and her pride towards it.

Comment: This structure reflects changing attitudes towards regional accents (see **page 76**).

The final word of the poem is "*home*", emphasising the importance of place to someone's identity.

Tone

The poem has a nostalgic tone, as the speaker reflects on memories they have of the subject. These memories are personal, which creates a sense of intimacy between the speaker and the reader.

The speaker is proud of the Midlands accent, and wants to "*shout it from the roofs*".

Language

Pride vs shame

Shame: The speaker addresses a subject who took "*hours*" of elocution lessons to repress their Midlands accent. It's hinted that the subject would be struck by the teacher if they spoke with their regional accent ("*the teacher's ruler across your legs*"). This suggests that speaking with a Midlands accent was 'bad' and deserved punishment.

> Corporal punishment (physical assault) was legal in UK schools up until 1986. Teachers were permitted to hit students, often with a cane or ruler, if the child misbehaved.

The speaker uses a **metaphor** of a box with a "*lock rusted shut*" to suggest that the subject's accent has been repressed for a long time. The box has been so firmly shut that it must be "*jemmied open*" (forced open with a crowbar) reinforcing how the subject was reluctant to speak with their accent because they were made to feel ashamed of it.

> **Comment:** Locked boxes often contain valuable or treasured objects. The symbolism of the subject locking their accent in a "*box beneath the bed*" could suggest that, although they repressed their accent, they also valued it and wanted to keep it safe.

Pride: The poem's speaker is proud of the Midlands accent, and is eager to "*lick*" and "*swallow*" all of its dialect words, suggesting that she wants the regional accent to be part of her. The **anaphora** of "*I wanted*" suggests the speaker's strong desire for a Midlands accent, and the phrase "*shout it from the roofs*" emphasises her pride.

> **Comment:** When the speaker clears the subject's house, the metaphorical locked box containing the subject's accent was the "*only*" thing she wanted. This emphasises its value to the speaker.

The different attitudes of the subject and the speaker towards the Midlands accent reflects the growing acceptance of, and pride towards, regional voices.

> **Comment:** It is implied that the speaker is eager to speak with a Midlands accent because it would allow them to feel closer to the subject. The speaker wants to "*swallow... the red brick / back-to-back you were born in*". This suggests that the Midlands accent reminds her of the subject, reinforcing the importance of language to a person's heritage and identity.

Language continued

Regional accent and dialect

The speaker creates a clear description of the Midlands accent using the phrases *"thick drawl"*, *"g's that rang"* and *"guttural uh"*.

Comment: The **consonance** in *"g's that rang"* and the **assonance** in *"guttural uh"* emphasise features of the Midlands accent which helps readers to imagine how it sounds.

The speaker describes how the accent would occasionally *"escape"*. The word *"escape"* associates the accent with freedom.

Homing also includes words from the Midlands dialect, including *"saft"*, *"blart"*, *"bibble, fettle, tay, wum"*. This makes the poem sound more authentic, and reinforces the speaker's pride.

Comment: The lively dialect words contrast with the monotonous phrase *"how now brown cow"*, emphasising how regional language is playful and creative.

Language associated with place

The speaker uses language linked to the Midlands' industrial past (see **page 76**) to reinforce its connection to her heritage.

 The **simile** *"vowels ferrous as nails"* and the **metaphor** *"my mouth, a blacksmith's furnace"* link the Midlands accent to iron production.

 The phrase *"consonants / you could lick the coal from"* links the Midlands accent to coal mining.

 The **onomatopoeic** words *"thunking and clanging"* help the reader imagine the sounds of the factories.

 The **triplet** of *"pits, / railways, factories"* clearly describes the Midlands' industrial landscape.

Comment: Factories are often presented negatively (particularly in this poetry cluster). However, in *Homing*, the speaker doesn't criticise them. Instead her descriptions emphasise her pride towards the Midlands' industrial past.

COMPARING *HOMING*

Here's how *Homing* could be compared to other poems.

 Remember, you can compare *Homing* with any poem from the anthology as long as your response is supported with examples. The following examples suggest ways to compare the poems, but they are not complete answers.

Representation of an industrial city

Homing presents the industrial area of the Midlands in a positive way. The speaker suggests that the local accent is intertwined with heavy industry, describing "*vowels as ferrous as nails*" and "*consonants / you could lick the coal from*". The anaphora of "*I wanted*" in relation to the Midlands accent suggests her strong desire to speak in a way that reflects the area's association with industry, for example, "*I wanted to swallow them all: the pits, / railways, factories*". The speaker's eagerness for a Midlands accent implies her positive feelings towards heavy industry in the area.

On the other hand, the speaker in *A Wider View* (**page 66**) presents the industrial city of Leeds in a more negative way. The speaker describes the "*smoke-filled sky*" which suggests the city is heavily polluted. They also describe the "*backyard*" of their great-great-grandfather's "*back-to-back*" and the repetition of "*back*" reinforces the sense of confinement living in an industrialised city.

Prejudice

Homing explores a person's experiences of prejudice in Britain. The subject in the poem takes "*hours*" of elocution lessons to disguise their Midlands accent. They are so ashamed of the way they speak that they hide their accent "*in a box beneath the bed*", and they are so reluctant to use their accent that the lock has "*rusted shut*". This hints at how regional accents were seen as inferior during the 20th century because they were associated with being working class, uneducated and poor. Elocution lessons provided an opportunity for people to hide their accent and be treated more fairly by middle- and upper- class society.

Thirteen (**page 122**) also explores experiences of prejudice, specifically racism in Britain. The speaker in the poem is just "*thirteen*" when he is stopped by police officers who suspect him of committing a robbery. The speaker emphasises his "*plump*" and youthful appearance to reinforce how ridiculous it was to be confused with the "*man*" who committed the crime. The speaker implies that he was apprehended because he was a young, black male, and the policemen associated his skin colour with criminality.

Compare how poets present ideas about belonging in *Homing* and in **one** other poem from Worlds and Lives. [30 marks]

Your answer may include:

AO1 — show understanding of the poems
- The speaker in 'Homing' explores her pride towards the Midlands, its industrial past and its distinctive accent and dialect. This suggests the speaker feels she belongs in the Midlands. On the other hand, the speaker in 'Like an Heiress' is initially excited to return to her home country of Guyana, however, when she sees a beach covered in rubbish, she feels ashamed and as though she no longer belongs there.

AO2 — show understanding of the poets' language choices
- Both poems explore feelings around pride and shame towards a place, and how that affects a person's sense of belonging. However, the poems explore these feelings of pride and shame in a different order. In 'Homing', the speaker begins by exploring a person's feelings of shame towards their regional accent. The subject metaphorically hides their accent "in a box beneath the bed", to try to distance themselves from the accent of their hometown. In 'Like an Heiress', the speaker is initially proud and excited to return to Guyana. She describes herself as an "heiress" which suggests that she is going to inherit something valuable on her trip, which reinforces her feelings of pride and belonging to Guyana.
- However, as the poems progress, they reverse their tones of pride of shame. In 'Homing', the poem ends with the speaker's pride towards the Midlands and its accent. She wanted to "shout it from the roofs", emphasising how she wants to celebrate her heritage. On the other hand, in 'Like an Heiress', when the speaker sees the rubbish on the beach she feels ashamed and as though she no longer belongs, describing herself as "tourist".
- Both poems use the first person to reflect how belonging is a personal experience. In 'Homing' the speaker uses anaphora, repeating the phrase "I wanted" to reinforce how she wanted to speak with a Midlands accent to feel as though she belongs to the area. In 'Like an Heiress', the speaker uses the first person to describe how visiting the beach makes her feel disconnected from Guyana. This makes the poem seem more intimate, which evokes feelings of sympathy from reader.

AO3 — relate the poems to the context
- Both poems could be autobiographical. Berry is from the Midlands, and her work often explores her regional identity. Similarly, Nichols has Guyanese heritage, and 'Like an Heiress' was inspired by a trip she took to Guyana.

This answer should be marked in accordance with the levels-based mark scheme on page 134.

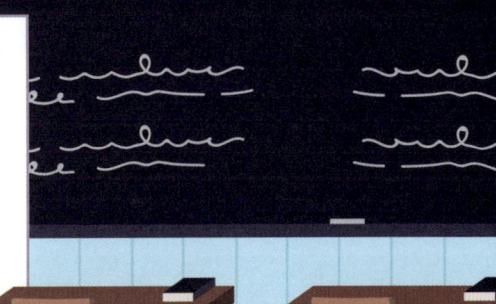

Make sure your answer to this question is in paragraphs and full sentences. Bullet points have been used in this example answer to suggest some information you could include.

We've included some quotes from *Like an Heiress* (**page 114**) in this sample answer, but direct quotes from the comparison poem aren't essential; you can use paraphrased examples or summaries to demonstrate your understanding.

A CENTURY LATER — IMTIAZ DHARKER

Going to school is compared to war. This introduces the idea that for some children, trying to get an education is dangerous.

The present tense makes the events of the poem seem more immediate.

The school-bell is a call to battle,
every step to class, a step into the firing-line.
Here is the target, fine skin at the temple,
cheek still rounded from being fifteen.

The description of the girl reinforces her youth, which suggests she is vulnerable.

"*surrounded*" emphasises the girl's powerlessness, and the sibilance creates an uneasy hissing sound.

5   Surrendered, surrounded, she
    takes the bullet in the head

Blunt language reinforces the brutality of the attack.

The enjambment across the stanza suggests that time has passed between the attack and the girl's recovery.

and walks on. The missile cuts
a pathway in her mind, to an orchard
in full bloom, a field humming under the sun,
10 its lap open and full of poppies.

The vibrant description suggests the girl's potential.

Poppies are associated with WWI, and symbolise death and remembrance.

This reinforces how unnecessary the attack was.

This girl has won
the right to be ordinary,

The determiner "*This*" implies that there are other girls who haven't won the right to be ordinary.

wear bangles to a wedding, paint her fingernails,
go to school. *Bullet, she says, you are stupid.*
15 *You have failed. You cannot kill a book*
or the buzzing *in it.*

The bullet is personified. This suggests that these words are aimed at the girl's attackers or anyone else who might attempt to use force to prevent girls from getting an education.

Onomatopoeic words create the sense of voices growing louder.

A murmur, a swarm. Behind her, one by one,
the schoolgirls are standing up
to take their places on the front line.

This reminds the reader of their youth and vulnerability.

The ending may trigger mixed emotions. Although readers may be optimistic that more girls are joining the fight for education, the phrase "*front line*" hints at the danger they continue to face.

Imtiaz Dharker

Imtiaz Dharker (b. 1954) was born in Pakistan but raised in Scotland. She is a poet, artist and film maker. *A century later* was published in 2014.

Imtiaz Dharker

Summary of the poem

The poem describes a 15-year-old girl who is shot in the head on her way to school. The girl survives the attack, and her courage inspires other schoolgirls to fight for their right to education.

Comment: The poem is based on the real-life attempted assassination of Pakistani schoolgirl, Malala Yousafzai, see **below**.

Context and references

Anthem for Doomed Youth and the First World War

Comment: The title of the poem, *A century later*, refers to the fact the poem was published in 2014, 100 years after the start of the First World War.

A century later was written as a response to another poem called *Anthem for Doomed Youth* by Wilfred Owen. *Anthem for Doomed Youth* criticises how the lives of young soldiers were cut unnecessarily short by the First World War (1914-1918). Both poems explore how violence can stop young people from reaching their full potential.

Comment: The opening line of *A century later* repeats ideas from the opening line of *Anthem for Doomed Youth*: "What passing-bells for those who die as cattle?"

A century later also refers to "*poppies*". Poppies became a symbol of remembrance of fallen soldiers following the First World War.

Malala Yousafzai

In 2012, Malala Yousafzai was 15 years old. She was on a school bus in the Swat Valley, Pakistan, when a member of the Taliban (a militant organisation that supports Islamic fundamentalism) boarded the bus and shot her in the head. Yousafzai was a vocal supporter of girls' education, and the Taliban wanted to silence her. Yousafzai survived the attack, and went on to become an education activist and won the Nobel Peace Prize in 2014.

The Nobel Prize is a prestigious award that is given to those who have made an enormous contribution to their field.

Malala Yousafzai

GCSE English Literature Poetry Anthology | Worlds and Lives

Themes

Oppression

The girls in the poem risk death every time they go to school. This reminds the reader of the oppression some girls face trying to get an education.

Form and structure

The poem is made up of six stanzas written in **free verse**. The first five stanzas alternate between quatrains and couplets, but the final stanza is a tercet (three-line stanza).

Comment: The irregular structure and lack of rhyme scheme or rhythm could represent the unpredictability faced by the girls every time they go to school.

The **enjambment** and line break between stanza two and stanza three suggests a time jump between the girl being shot and being able to "*walk on*". This reinforces the girl's determination to keep fighting for education.

The poem is written in the **present tense** which makes the events described seem more immediate.

Comment: Using the present tense also reflects how educational oppression is an ongoing problem for girls in many parts of the world.

The poem is narrated by a speaker in the third person. However, in the fifth stanza, the reader hears from the girl via **direct speech**, which is signalled using **italics**.

Comment: The narrator gives the girl a voice, which reinforces how her attackers have failed to silence her.

The first five stanzas focus on the individual girl, her attack and her resilience. However, the final stanza describes how the girl's bravery has inspired others. This suggests that education activism is gaining momentum, but the phrase "*front line*" and its association with warfare hints at the danger schoolgirls continue to face everyday.

Tone

The poem opens with an uneasy tone by comparing going to school with going into battle.

The poem is inspirational, describing the strength and resilience of the girl following her attack.

Comment: The poem may make some readers feel grateful that they can attend school without the fear of violence.

The poem ends with a hopeful tone, describing how other schoolgirls are *"standing up / to take their places on the front line"*. This suggests that girls will continue to fight for their education.

Comment: Although this creates hope, it's also tragic that girls have to put themselves at risk for this basic right.

Language

Language of war

The poem uses military language to reinforce the violence faced by some girls who want an education.

In the first stanza, the speaker uses the **metaphor** *"The school-bell is a call to battle"* and they compare walking to class as a *"step into the firing-line"*. The **juxtaposition** of education and warfare creates a shocking opening.

The girl **personifies** the bullet in the fifth stanza, calling it *"stupid"* and telling it *"You have failed"*. The personification suggests that the girl's words are directed at her attackers, or anyone else prepared to use violence against schoolgirls.

The final stanza describes how the schoolgirls *"take their places on the front line"*. In war zones, the front line is where the battle is fought and the highest number of casualties occur. This reinforces the girls' bravery, but also the danger they face.

Language continued

Representation of the girl

Young

The speaker emphasises the girl's youth. She has "*fine skin*" and a "*rounded*" cheek, suggesting a child-like appearance, which reinforces her innocence and vulnerability. She is also referred to as a "*girl*", which implies she is just a child.

Comment: Emphasising the girl's youth makes the attack even more shocking.

Courageous

Despite being shot in the head, the girl is determined to carry on fighting for girls' right to education. She bravely states: "*You have failed. You cannot kill a book*".

Comment: The **caesura** in this line reinforces the girl's defiant attitude.

Promising

The girl's mind is described using the **metaphor** "*an orchard / in full bloom*". Apples are often associated with knowledge, so comparing her mind to an "*orchard*" suggests her intelligence and potential.

Comment: The beautiful natural imagery used to describe the girl's mind contrasts with the unpleasant imagery of war and violence.

Relatable

She is presented as a typical teenager. She wears "*bangles*" and paints "*her fingernails*". This makes her relatable: she could be any teenage girl.

Comment: The description of her "*ordinary*" teenage behaviour reminds the reader how some girls have to fight to do things that others take for granted.

Inspirational

Other girls stand "*Behind her*", suggesting that she has inspired them to fight for their right to education.

Comment: The schoolgirls' determination reinforces that education is a cause worth fighting for.

Language continued

Representation of the attackers

Cruel

The attackers describe the girl as "*the target*" which suggests they don't consider her a human being. This reinforces their brutality.

Comment: The attack doesn't stop the girl, and it encourages other girls to stand up for their rights. This reinforces the futility of their violence.

Cowardly

The attackers "*surrounded*" the girl, which suggests she was outnumbered. This presents the attackers as cowardly: they sent several people to kill an unarmed 15-year-old schoolgirl.

Comment: The **sibilance** in the phrase "*Surrendered, surrounded*" creates a hissing sound which creates an uneasy atmosphere as the attackers approach the girl.

Onomatopoeic language

The speaker uses **onomatopoeia** throughout the poem, for example "*humming*", "*buzzing*", "*murmur*" and "*swarm*". The words could suggest a building of voices as people begin to speak out against the injustice of the attack and the girls' right to education.

Comparison to bees

Describing the girls as a "*swarm*" likens them to bees.

Bees are small, but they have a powerful sting. This could hint at the surprising strength of the schoolgirls.

Colonies of bees are led by a queen: a powerful female. This could refer to the girl who was shot who has inspired the other girls around her.

Bees are colony insects: individually they have little power, but they work collectively to achieve their aims. This mirrors how the schoolgirls fight for their rights together.

GCSE English Literature Poetry Anthology | Worlds and Lives

COMPARING *A CENTURY LATER*

Here's how *A century later* could be compared to other poems.

 Remember, you can compare *A century later* with any poem from the anthology as long as your response is supported with examples. The following examples suggest ways to compare the poems, but they are not complete answers.

Education and violence

A century later explores how girls are oppressed in some countries because they are denied the right to an education. The first stanza uses military language to emphasise the violence that some schoolgirls face, using a metaphor to describe the school bell as "*a call to battle*" and walking into class as a "*step into the firing line*". Education is usually presented positively, so likening it to warfare creates a shocking opening to the poem. This may make readers feel grateful that they didn't have to put themselves at risk to receive an education.

Homing (see **page 74**) also includes images of violence in the classroom. The speaker describes how the subject of the poem had elocution lessons to try to hide her Midlands accent. The teacher would strike a "*ruler*" across the subject's legs if they spoke incorrectly. This presents the elocution lessons as harsh and unforgiving, and suggests that speaking with an accent was a punishable offence. This may make readers appreciate that corporal punishment is no longer acceptable in schools, and attitudes towards regional accents have changed: they are now celebrated, rather than punished.

Highlighting injustice

Dharker uses *A century later* to highlight the injustice faced by young girls who are denied access to education. She uses the real-life story of education activist Malala Yousafzai who was shot in the head because she spoke out against the Taliban's oppression of girls. The speaker presents the gunmen as cowardly, as they "*surrounded*" the girl, suggesting the Taliban sent several men to kill an unarmed school girl. The speaker presents their actions as futile, stating "*Bullet… You have failed*", which gives the reader hope that violence will not deter the girls from trying to attend school.

Khan uses *pot* (see **pages 58–59**) to highlight the injustice of Europeans who took artefacts from the countries they colonised. She presents these colonisers as "*looters*", reinforcing how they stole the pot from Nigeria. She imagines the made-up excuses they gave for possessing the pot, such as it slipping on to their "*yacht*" or that it was "*lost*". This presents the colonisers as liars, and the phrase "*finders keepers*" trivialises their actions, and suggests that they have no remorse. Both poems call for change. *A century later* wants to end the oppression of girls, and *pot* calls for museums to return items that were unlawfully taken from other countries.

Compare how poets present ideas about oppression in *A century later* and in **one** other poem from Worlds and Lives. [30 marks]

Your answer may include:

AO1 — show understanding of the poems

- Both 'A century later' and 'Thirteen' explore ideas about oppression. In 'A century later', the speaker focuses on a girl who was shot in the head because she believed girls have a right to receive an education. This highlights how men in some parts of the world oppress girls. In 'Thirteen', the speaker describes being stopped by police when he was a teenager and accused of committing a robbery. The speaker implies that the police suspected him because he was a young, black male, highlighting the issue of racism in British law enforcement.

AO2 — show understanding of the poets' language choices

- Both poets create sympathy for the victims by emphasising their youth. In 'A century later', the girl is described as having a "rounded" cheek. This suggests her face is full, hinting at a child-like appearance. Similarly, in 'Thirteen', the boy is described as "plump" which suggests that he doesn't have the strong, muscular body of an adult. In both poems, the victims' appearance highlights how young and unthreatening they are, which makes the oppression they experience seem even more shocking and unnecessary.

- Both poets present the victims as promising. In 'A century later', the girl's mind is described as an "orchard / in full bloom". Apples are associated with knowledge, so this suggests she is intelligent, and the connotations of blossom suggest her potential is developing and flourishing. Similarly, the speaker in 'Thirteen' and his classmates are described as the "biggest and brightest stars". This suggests they have bright futures ahead of them. Both poems present the victims as promising to highlight how oppression can destroy a young person's potential.

- Both poems have a pessimistic ending. In 'A century later', the final lines of the poem describe the "schoolgirls" taking "their places on the front line" to suggest that girls are standing up for their right to education. The phrase "front line" implies that they are putting themselves in danger and they will continue to be oppressed by those who want to prevent them from receiving an education. Similarly, in 'Thirteen', the speaker ends the poem with a description of "dying stars / on the verge of becoming black holes". This ending links back to the earlier description of the speaker as a star, and the word "dying" suggests that racism can destroy someone's potential. The phrase "black holes" suggests that experiences of prejudice can leave people feeling empty. Both poems highlight how oppression negatively affects people's lives.

AO3 — relate the poems to the context

- Both poems are based on real-life experiences which remind the reader that oppression still occurs. 'A century later' is based on the experiences of Malala Yousafzai who was shot in the head by Taliban gunmen. 'Thirteen' is based on Femi's own experiences of being stopped by police for a crime he didn't commit.

This answer should be marked in accordance with the levels-based mark scheme on page 134.

Make sure your answer to this question is in paragraphs and full sentences. Bullet points have been used in this example answer to suggest some information you could include.

We've included some quotes from *Thirteen* (**page 122**) in this sample answer, but direct quotes from the comparison poem aren't essential; you can use paraphrased examples or summaries to demonstrate your understanding.

THE JEWELLERY MAKER — LOUISA ADJOA PARKER

Each day after sunrise he walks to the workshop
– like his father before him, and his father too –
the slap of sandalled feet on heat-baked stone,
the smell of blossom, a plate-blue sky. He greets
5 his neighbours with a smile. In the distance
a wild dog barks.

He sits straight-backed, lays out pointed tools
the way a surgeon might – neat as soldiers.
He likes hot metal, the smell, the way it yields
10 to his touch. Under deft fingers gold butterflies dance;
flowers bloom; silvery moons wax and wane,
then wax again; bright dragonflies flap two pairs of wings.

He likes the tiny loops and curls – he'd decorate
his house in this, drape his wife in fine-spun gold;
15 her skin wrinkled by sun, in simple cotton dress,
her only jewellery a plain gold band, worn thin.
He imagines the women who will wear
what he has made, clear-eyed, bird-boned, unlined skin
warming the metal his hands caress.

Annotations:

- The jewellery maker goes to work early in the morning, which suggests he works long hours.
- This suggests his workshop is close by, implying he lives and works within a small, local area.
- This suggests the jewellery maker's life is familiar but repetitive.
- This suggests the poem is set somewhere hot and rural.
- His craft has been passed down through generations, and is an important part of his heritage.
- Sensory language describes what he can hear, smell and see which creates a vivid sense of place.
- This reinforces the jewellery maker's skill and precision.
- The man's posture suggests he takes his work seriously.
- This makes him seem almost God-like in his ability to create, but also suggests he is inspired by his surroundings.
- Dynamic verbs suggest his creations are realistic.
- This suggests the man and his wife are poor. Her "*plain gold band*" contrasts with the elaborate jewellery he makes for other women.
- He longs to give his wife a better life.
- The description of the women suggests that they could have a European appearance.
- This suggests the man puts a lot of love and care into the pieces he makes. He may be imagining that he is making the jewellery for his wife, or it could hint his customers will not appreciate the pieces as much as he does.
- This contrasts with the wife's "*wrinkled*" skin, suggesting the women who buy his jewellery have an easier life.

Louisa Adjoa Parker

Louisa Adjoa Parker (b. 1972) is a writer of British-Ghanaian heritage who currently lives in England. Her poetry often focuses on marginalised voices, and explores themes including racism, identity, home and place. She writes and speaks about mental health, and how her own mental health has been impacted by belonging to marginalised groups. *The Jewellery Maker* was published in 2018 in her collection *Filigree*.

Louisa Adjoa Parker

Summary of the poem

The poem begins by describing a jewellery maker as he walks to his workshop. The man is presented as highly skilled, and he makes beautiful and delicate objects out of gold for wealthy customers. Despite his skill, it's hinted that the jewellery maker and his wife are poor.

Context and references

Ghana

Ghana is a country in Africa and is one of the world's largest producers of gold. Between 1821–1957, Ghana was colonised by Britain, and was known as Gold Coast. The British government controlled gold mining in the area, and diverted wealth to Britain, away from Ghana.

Comment: Although it's not clear where the poem is set, it could take place in Ghana where the poet's family are from. The poverty of the jewellery maker could be a criticism of colonial control of gold in Ghana.

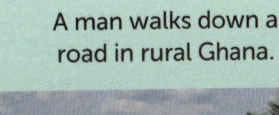

A man walks down a road in rural Ghana.

Craftsmanship

Traditionally, certain trades, such as goldsmithing, were passed down through generations of the same family. However, the development of factory production means that lots of items which were commonly made by hand are now mass produced. Mass production allows companies to charge less for their products because they are made more cheaply. This has put some craftspeople out of business because they cannot compete with the low prices of mass production, so some traditional skills are dying out.

Comment: The jewellery maker works "*Each day*" and creates each of his objects individually by hand. Despite the time, skill and materials involved, he is not wealthy. This suggests he is not paid fairly for the work that he does.

GCSE English Literature Poetry Anthology | Worlds and Lives

Themes

Identity
The man's craft has been passed down through generations. This suggests his skill with gold is an important part of his heritage and identity.

Belonging
The jewellery maker "*greets / his neighbours with a smile*". This suggests that he belongs to the local community.

Oppression
The jewellery maker is highly skilled and works with precious metal to make beautiful objects. However, it is implied that he doesn't earn much money, suggesting that his customers do not pay him fairly for his work, which keeps him poor.

Form and structure

The poem is told by an omniscient narrator (a narrator who knows everything). It is written in the **third person** in the **present tense**, and the use of **free verse** and **enjambment** add to the story-like quality of the poem.

Comment: The fluid structure could also reflect the confident and assured way the man works.

The long sentences slow the **pace** of the poem and help create a calm, reflective tone.

The poem is split into three stanzas. The first two stanzas **chronologically** describe the man's journey to work and his daily routine. The final stanza explores the thoughts and feelings of the man as he works.

Comment: Exploring the man's thoughts and feelings develops his character which allows the reader to understand him better. This creates a connection between the man and the reader.

The poem contains a lot of **caesura**. This interrupts the flow of the poem, and could hint at difficulties in the jewellery maker's life, such as his frustration that he cannot afford to give his wife the life he thinks she deserves.

Tone

The Jewellery Maker has a calm tone. The man works in a controlled, unhurried way, which allows him to create beautiful objects.

The poem has an underlying tone of irony. It's ironic that the jewellery maker works with precious metal, but it's implied that he could only afford a *"plain gold band"* for his wife. This hints that the man is underpaid, despite the value of the jewellery he makes.

Language

Representation of the location

Although the location isn't identified, the speaker uses **sensory language** to create a vivid scene. This creates a sense of familiarity which emphasises how the man belongs to the area.

 "the smell of blossom"

 "heat-baked stone"

 "a plate-blue sky"

 "the slap of sandalled feet"

Comment: The **onomatopoeic** word *"slap"* and the **sibilance** creates a clear sound of the jewellery maker's footsteps.

Representation of the man's work

The speaker also uses **sensory language** to describe the man's work which helps the reader understand the skill and effort involved in the jewellery maker's work.

"the smell" of *"hot metal"* | the way the gold *"yields / to his touch"* | *"pointed tools"*

Language continued

Representation of the jewellery maker

Comment: The jewellery maker isn't given a name and the reader doesn't hear him speak. This could reflect how poor and marginalised people aren't given a voice in society. Referring to him only as "*The Jewellery Maker*" also emphasises how important his craft is to his identity.

Hard-working

He goes to work "*Each day after sunrise*" which suggests he gets up early and works every day.

Comment: Although this presents the jewellery maker as hard-working, it could also suggest that he has to work long hours to provide for his family.

Proud

The jewellery maker takes pride in his work: he "*sits straight-backed*" and lays out his tools in a "*neat*" way. This suggests his work is important to him.

Creative

The speaker uses dynamic verbs to describe the jewellery maker's creations. They "*dance*", "*bloom*" and "*flap*". This suggests he is creative and his work is life-like.

Skilful

The jewellery maker is compared to a "*surgeon*", a job which requires years of training and a high level of skill. He is also described as having "*deft fingers*", which suggests his precision.

Comment: It's implied that the jewellery maker learnt his craft from his father, and the skills have been passed down through generations. This suggests that making jewellery is an important part of his family identity.

Aspirational

He imagines decorating his house with "*loops and curls*" of gold, and making "*fine-spun*" jewellery for his wife. This suggests he dreams of a better life for his family.

Enjoys his job

The jewellery maker seems to enjoy his job. The speaker repeats the phrase "*He likes*" to describe the "*hot metal*" and "*the tiny loops and curls*".

Language continued

Contrasts between the wife and the customers

The final stanza **juxtaposes** the jewellery maker's wife with the women who wear his jewellery. This highlight the differences between them.

The wife has "*skin wrinkled by the sun*". This suggests that she works outside, possibly doing a manual job.

The women who buy the jewellery have "*unlined skin*", suggesting they are young or do not work outdoors in the sun. This suggests they lead easier lives.

Comment: The customers are "*clear-eyed*" and "*bird-boned*". This could suggest they have light-coloured eyes and a narrow bone structure: features more typical in Europeans. The speaker could be implying that white people exploit the jewellery maker, and do not pay him fairly for his work.

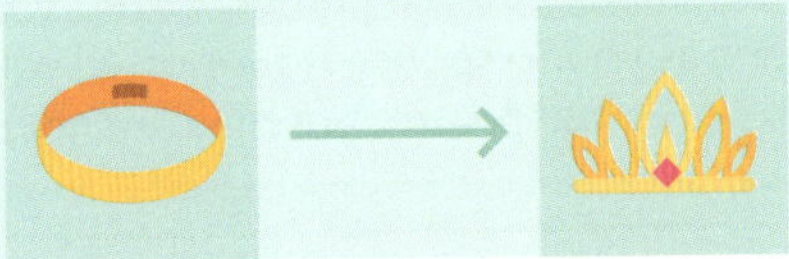

The wife wears "*a plain gold band, worn thin*". This suggests he could only afford a simple wedding ring and he cannot afford to repair it. However, the phrase "*worn thin*" suggests they have been married for a long time, so the ring symbolises their love and commitment.

Comment: She also wears a "*simple cotton dress*", which reinforces their lack of wealth.

The customers buy jewellery decorated with "*flowers*" and "*butterflies*", suggesting they can afford ornate, elaborate pieces. Their jewellery symbolises their wealth and status.

COMPARING *THE JEWELLERY MAKER*

Here's how *The Jewellery Maker* could be compared to other poems.

 Remember, you can compare *The Jewellery Maker* with any poem from the anthology as long as your response is supported with examples. The following examples suggest ways to compare the poems, but they are not complete answers.

Language of contrasts

The speaker in *The Jewellery Maker* uses contrasting language to compare the man's wife to the women who buy his jewellery to emphasise the division between them. In one example, the speaker describes the wife's "*plain gold*" wedding ring, which suggests that the jewellery maker could only afford a simple ring. This contrasts with the elaborate "*loops and curls*" decorating the jewellery for his customers. This highlights the wealth and status of the man's customers in comparison to his own lack of money.

The speaker in *On an Afternoon Train...* (see **pages 42–43**) uses contrasting language to show how disconnected he feels from his home in Jamaica. The speaker compares the "*lit*" streets in London to his father's banana field in "*darkness*". This suggests that he struggles to remember Jamaica clearly, which highlights how far away it seems to him. Similarly, the Quaker comments that Jamaica is a "*sunny*" country, however, the speaker can only think about "*Snow*", suggesting that he struggles to remember the warmth of Jamaica, and can only feel the chill of England.

Place

Although the country that the poem is set in is never identified, the speaker in *The Jewellery Maker* creates a vivid sense of place for the reader. They do this using sensory language to describe what the jewellery maker can see, touch, smell and hear. The speaker describes the *slap of sandalled feet*", and the onomatopoeic word "*slap*" along with the sibilance create a clear sound of the man's feet hitting the ground. It is easy for the reader to imagine the warmth radiating from the "*heat-baked stone*" and the fragrant smell of "*blossom*". This description also adds to the comforting tone in the poem, as the speaker is familiar with the route he takes "*Each day*" to his workshop.

The speaker in *Lines Written in Early Spring* (see **page 10**) also creates a vivid sense of place using sensory language. The speaker describes hearing "*a thousand blended notes*", and the soothing sound of birdsong, along with the sensation of the "*breezy air*", creates a peaceful and relaxing tone. This helps to immerse the reader in the "*grove*" where the speaker is sitting, and reinforces the beauty and harmony found in nature.

Compare how poets present ideas about identity in *The Jewellery Maker* and in **one** other poem from Worlds and Lives. [30 marks]

Your answer may include:

AO1 — show understanding of the poems

- Both 'The Jewellery Maker' and 'pot' explore the importance of purpose, family and place on a person's identity. 'The Jewellery Maker' examines the routine of a goldsmith whose craft has been passed down through generations of the same family, and how his occupation has shaped his identity. 'pot' focuses on an artefact which was taken by European colonists from its home country of Nigeria, and how this displacement has affected the pot's identity.

AO2 — show understanding of the poets' language choices

- Both speakers suggest that having a purpose is important to a person's identity. In 'The Jewellery Maker', the reader never learns the man's name: he is only referred to as 'The Jewellery Maker', showing the importance of his profession to his identity. The man's job brings him a sense of purpose, as "He likes" working with gold. However, in 'pot', the speaker reflects that the pot is "empty" rather than full of "warm grain". This suggests that the pot is unfulfilled because it is on display in a museum rather having a purpose.

- Both speakers suggest that family is important to a person's identity. The man in 'The Jewellery Maker' has learnt his profession from "his father before him, and his father too", reinforcing how his job connects him to past generations. In 'pot', the speaker recalls returning to where her "family's from". She presents this experience positively, commenting that they "laughed a lot".

- Both poems suggest that traditional crafts are an important way for a person to express their cultural identity. In 'The Jewellery Maker', the man makes beautiful handmade gold objects, and he caresses the gold, which reinforces the love and care he puts into each of his pieces. The man takes inspiration from the world around him, making "dragonflies" and "butterflies" suggesting that his creativity is inspired by his environment. In 'pot', the speaker describes how the pot was made by hand ("finger nails / pressed") and that the pot was "loved" by the people who made it. The person who made the pot decorated it with a "snake" pattern, suggesting that they were also inspired by the world around them.

AO3 — relate the poems to the context

- Both poets may have drawn on their own cultural identities in their poems. Adjoa Parker is of Ghanaian descent, and Ghana is one of the world's leading producers of gold, so 'The Jewellery Maker' may celebrate the skill and craftsmanship of goldsmiths in Ghana. Khan is of Pakistani heritage, and Pakistan was an English colony. This allows her to empathise with the Nigerian pot, because Nigeria was also a British colony.

This answer should be marked in accordance with the levels-based mark scheme on page 134.

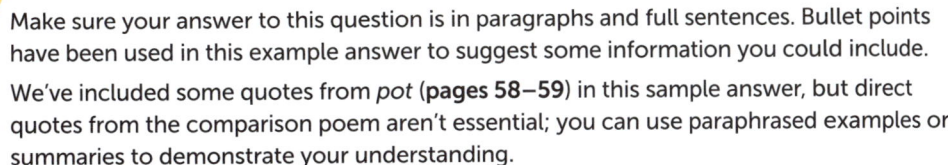

Make sure your answer to this question is in paragraphs and full sentences. Bullet points have been used in this example answer to suggest some information you could include.

We've included some quotes from *pot* (**pages 58–59**) in this sample answer, but direct quotes from the comparison poem aren't essential; you can use paraphrased examples or summaries to demonstrate your understanding.

GCSE English Literature Poetry Anthology | Worlds and Lives

WITH BIRDS YOU'RE NEVER LONELY — RAYMOND ANTROBUS

This introduces the difficulties that some deaf people experience trying to communicate in loud environments. → I can't hear the barista ← **The poem starts in the middle of the action which reflects the speaker's sense of confusion and disorientation at not being able to hear the barista.**

over the coffee machine.

Spoons slam, steam rises. ← **Sibilance and onomatopoeia emphasise the noisy cafe and the hissing of the steam.**

I catch the eye of a man

The man is reading about trees, rather than experiencing them. This suggests that living in a city creates distance between humans and nature.

5   sitting in the corner

of the cafe reading alone ← **The speaker repeats the word "alone" which creates a shared experience between him and the man, and introduces ideas about loneliness.**

→ about trees which is, incidentally,

→ all I can think about

The speaker longs to reconnect with nature, which suggests he feels disconnected from his urban environment.

since returning.

10   Last week I sat alone ← **The poem shifts to a memory, so the speaker switches to the past tense.**

→ on a stump, deep in Zelandia forest

"deep" suggests the forest is far from civilisation.

with sun-syrupped Kauri trees ← **The beautiful imagery suggests the trees are glowing with warmth and light.**

Nature is presented as colourful and vibrant.

→ and brazen Tui birds with white tufts

→ and yellow and black beaks.

15   They landed by my feet, blaring so loudly

Tui birds can replicate sounds found in urban environments such as human voices, car alarms or music. The noise made by the Tui may have reminded the speaker of the urban noises he wants to escape from.

→ I had to turn off my hearing aids.

When all sound disappeared, I was tuned ← **The speaker is able to connect with the forest once he is no longer overwhelmed by the sound of the birds.**

into a silence that was not an absence.

"*silence collapsed*" and "*spat*" suggests being able to hear again was unpleasant.

As I switched sound on again,
20 silence collapsed.

The speaker can precisely remember the smell ("*earthy*"), colour and sensation ("*sturdiness*") of the trees. This suggests that they made a strong impression on him.

The forest spat all the birds back,
and I was jealous—

the earthy Kauri trees, their endless
brown and green trunks of sturdiness.

This refers to the book about trees the man reads in the cafe. The speaker hints at the irony that humans cut down trees to make books about trees, which reinforces how humans are becoming disconnected from nature.

25 I wondered what the trees would say about us?
What books would they write if they had to cut us down?

The rhetorical question reminds the reader how humans damage nature.

This suggests the speaker was disorientated when he left the forest.

Later, stumbling from the forest I listened
to a young Maori woman.

Unlike the speaker, the Maori woman isn't overwhelmed by the birdsong.

She could tell which bird chirped,
30 a skill she learned from her grandfather

Suggests that connecting with nature is an important aspect of Maori culture.

Being in nature can bring people comfort. This repeats the poem's title which reinforces its significance.

who said with birds you're never lonely.
In that moment I felt sorry

"*grey*" contrasts with the "*green*" of the Kauri trees, and the "*white*", "*yellow*" and "*black*" tui birds, suggesting that nature cannot thrive in urban environments.

for any grey tree in London,
for the family they don't have,
35 the Gods they can't hold.

The London tree is presented as being by itself rather than in a "*forest*" like the Kauri trees. This suggests that urbanisation has negatively impacted nature.

The poem is structured in couplets apart from this final line. This could reflect the loneliness of city life.

This line is ambiguous, but it could suggest that being in an urban environment can make it harder to connect with God.

GCSE English Literature Poetry Anthology | Worlds and Lives

Raymond Antrobus

Raymond Antrobus (b. 1986) is a British poet with Jamaican heritage. He is deaf, so he often explores sound, communication and connection in his poetry. *With Birds You're Never Lonely* was published in 2019.

Raymond Antrobus

Summary of the poem

The speaker is in a noisy cafe and he sees a man reading a book about trees. This reminds the speaker of a recent trip to New Zealand, where he sat in a forest listening to birds. The birds were so loud the speaker had to turn his hearing aids off. When he leaves the forest, he listens to a Maori woman who can identity birds from their calls. The speaker reflects on nature and feels sorry for the trees in London.

Context and references

New Zealand

In the poem, the speaker has just returned from "*Zealandia*", which refers to a piece of continental crust which is largely submerged under water. Where the crust is above sea level, it creates several islands including New Zealand and New Caledonia.

The poem describes species which are native to New Zealand: the tui bird and the kauri tree.

Tui birds have very unusual and distinctive birdsong. They can also replicate man-made sounds such as speech and car alarms.

A tui bird

The poem refers to a "*Maori woman*". Maori are indigenous people of New Zealand, and their culture believes in living in harmony with nature and treating it with respect.

Comment: The Maori woman in the poem can recognise different birdsong. This reflects how she is attuned to nature.

Left: A kauri tree   Right: A Maori woman

The speaker describes kauri trees as having "*endless*" trunks. Kauri are some of the tallest trees in the world, growing up to 50 metres high.

Themes

Loneliness

The speaker sees a man in the cafe "*alone*" and later describes how he also sat "*alone*". He also feels sorry for "*any grey tree in London, / for the family they don't have*".

Nature

The poem explores the speaker's relationship with nature.

Environmental damage

The speaker suggests that humankind negatively impacts nature. Humans "*cut*" down trees, and urbanisation has made the trees in London "*grey*".

Form and structure

With Birds You're Never Lonely is written in **couplets**, which could reinforce the poem's ideas about humans and nature living alongside each other in harmony.

Comment: The exception to the couplet structure is the final line which stands alone. This line could represent the isolation felt by the solitary trees in urban environments.

The poem is written in **free verse** and the lines are often **enjambed**. This more closely resembles natural speech, and clearly presents the voice of the speaker.

Comment: The poem shares some similarities with **monologues**: it is written in the first person, and explores the speaker's inner thoughts and feelings.

The poem begins in the **present tense** and the speaker describes a noisy cafe where he sees a customer reading a book about trees. This triggers memories of a trip the speaker took to New Zealand, and this **flashback** is signalled by the speaker switching to the **past tense**. Reflecting on memories of New Zealand's natural beauty saddens the speaker, as he considers the effects of urbanisation on nature in London.

Comment: The speaker's reflective tone is reinforced by his use of **rhetorical questions**, as he wonders what nature thinks of humans.

Tone

The speaker is overwhelmed at several points in the poem. In the cafe, he "*can't hear the barista*", and in the forest he turns off his hearing aids because of the birds. He is described as "*stumbling*" out of the forest, suggesting he feels disorientated.

The poem has a thoughtful and reflective tone. The speaker considers humankind's relationship with nature, and reflects that nature and humans thrive when they co-exist peacefully in rural environments.

Language

Representation of the speaker

Overwhelmed

The speaker seems overwhelmed by city life: he can't hear the barista over the noise of the cafe.

Preoccupied by nature

Nature is all the speaker "*can think about*", which suggests that his experiences in New Zealand have had a profound impact on him.

Self-aware

The speaker recognises the damage that humans do to the environment. Humans cut down trees for paper and urbanise environments which makes it difficult for nature to thrive. The speaker feels sorry for nature and tries to imagine the world from its perspective.

Comment: In the final line of the poem, the speaker feels sorry for city trees and "*the Gods they can't hold*". This line is ambiguous, but it could suggest that trees which grow in urban environments lose a spiritual connection to the world around them.

Noise and silence

The speaker contrasts descriptions of noise and silence.

The cafe is presented as noisy. The speaker can't hear the barista over the coffee machine and he describes how "*Spoons slam, steam rises*". This suggests that being in the cafe is unpleasant and overwhelming.

Comment: The **onomatopoeic** word "*slam*" reinforces the noise, and the **sibilance** in the phrase mimics the hissing sound made by the coffee machine.

In the forest, the birds are described as "*blaring*" which suggests the sound they make is loud and harsh. The speaker is so overwhelmed by the noise he turns off his hearing aids.

Hearing aids allow those with hearing impairments pick up sound more clearly. However, some hearing aids amplify all noise, making it difficult for wearers to distinguish speech from background noise which can be overwhelming.

Comment: The poem helps readers who are not hearing impaired understand the difficulties faced by those with hearing difficulties, and how everyday activities such as visiting a cafe or listening to birdsong can be challenging.

When the speaker turns off his hearing aids, "*all sound disappeared*". This allows him to become "*tuned / into*" the silence, which suggests he feels connected to the forest.

Language continued

Representation of urban and rural environments

The speaker contrasts his experiences in London with his experiences in the New Zealand forest, and suggests that urbanisation has negatively affected both nature and humans. The speaker seems disconnected from urban life, presenting it as isolating, overwhelming and colourless, whereas being in the forest is comforting, peaceful and colourful. This suggests that when humans and nature respectfully co-exist, everyone benefits.

In London: The man in the cafe sits "*alone*" and the speaker suggests trees in the city don't have any "*family*". This presents city life as isolating.

In the forest: The speaker is "*alone*" in the forest but the tui birds approach him, and the poem's title, *With Birds You're Never Lonely*, suggests the speaker finds companionship in nature.

In London: The man in the cafe reads a book about trees, which hints that this is the only way he can experience nature.

Comment: The speaker hints at the irony that humans cut down trees to make books about trees, reinforcing how humans have become disconnected from nature.

In the forest: The speaker was "*deep*" in nature. He is "*jealous*" of the kauri trees, perhaps because they live far from human civilisation.

In London: The tree is "*grey*", suggesting nature is weak and colourless in the city.

In the forest: The kauri trees are "*sun-syrupped*", suggesting they glow in the sunlight. This presents nature as warm and inviting. The speaker admires their "*sturdiness*" implying the trees in the forest are strong.

In London: The speaker is overwhelmed by the sounds of the cafe, but he doesn't turn off his hearing aids, suggesting that he has to endure the noise to be part of society.

In the forest: When the speaker is overwhelmed by the tui birds, he can turn off his hearing aids and enjoy the silence.

Comment: The Maori woman isn't overwhelmed by the birds because her grandfather taught her how to identify their song. This suggests that nature is an important part of her cultural identity. She also symbolises how humans are capable of living in harmony with nature.

COMPARING *WITH BIRDS YOU'RE NEVER LONELY*

Here's how *With Birds You're Never Lonely* could be compared to other poems.

 Remember, you can compare *With Birds You're Never Lonely* with any poem from the anthology as long as your response is supported with examples. The following examples suggest ways to compare the poems, but they are not complete answers.

Memories of place

The speaker in *With Birds You're Never Lonely* longs to return to New Zealand. The poem begins with the speaker in a cafe, but all he "*can think about*" are the trees in New Zealand. He notices a man reading a book about trees, and this transports the speaker back to the New Zealand forest. The memory of New Zealand is vivid for the speaker, as he is able to describe the "*earthy*" smell and "*brown and green trunks*" of the kauri trees with precision, suggesting that they made a lasting impression on him.

The speaker in *On an Afternoon Train…* (**pages 42–43**) also uses memories to show how a speaker longs for a place. The speaker has a conversation with a Quaker which "*Inexplicably*" triggers memories of his home in Jamaica, and his "*father's big banana field*". However, the banana field is "*in darkness*" which suggests that the memory feels distant, reinforcing how far the speaker feels from his home country.

Monologues

With Birds You're Never Lonely shares some features with a monologue: it is written in the first person and explores the personal thoughts and feelings of the speaker. The poem's use of free verse and enjambment also more closely follow the patterns of natural speech, which adds to its conversational style. The speaker is likely to be the poet, Raymond Antrobus, as he describes his experiences of deafness, including feeling overwhelmed by sound, and difficulties hearing the barista over the noise in the cafe. The autobiographical nature of the poem allows the reader to develop a closer bond with the poet.

Name Journeys (see **pages 50–51**) also shares features with monologues, and mimics natural speech using free verse and enjambment. It is also an autobiographical poem which explores Raman Mundair's experiences of immigrating from India to Manchester as a child, and the difficulties that she faced trying to integrate into British culture, whilst also trying to retain her cultural heritage. Mundair's honest account of immigration allows the reader to sympathise with her and reflect on their own treatment of those who have experienced displacement.

Compare how poets present nature in *With Birds You're Never Lonely* and in **one** other poem from Worlds and Lives.

[30 marks]

Your answer may include:

AO1 — show understanding of the poems

- Both 'With Birds You're Never Lonely' and 'Lines Written in Early Spring' present nature as calming and relaxing. However, both speakers suggest that humankind has a negative impact on the world around them.

AO2 — show understanding of the poets' language choices

- Both speakers suggest that nature is beautiful. The speaker in 'With Birds You're Never Lonely' presents nature in New Zealand as colourful, describing the "white", "yellow" and "black" of the tui birds, and the "green" of the kauri trees. This helps the reader clearly picture the vibrant scene. The speaker in 'Lines Written in Early Spring' also creates a vivid image of nature's beauty using sensory language. The speaker describes the sound of "a thousand blended notes", the sensation of the "breezy air" and the sight of the "green bower".

- Both speakers suggest a connection between nature and spirituality. The speaker in 'With Birds You're Never Lonely' suggests that trees which grow in the city are disconnected from "Gods". This implies that being in a rural environment brings people closer to God. Similarly, the speaker in 'Lines Written in Early Spring' uses language associated with religion when talking about nature, such as "soul", "faith" and "heaven". This reinforces the idea that being in nature is a spiritual experience.

- Both speakers suggest that humankind disrupts the harmony found in nature. In 'With Birds You're Never Lonely', the speaker ironically recalls how humans cut down trees to make books about trees. This suggests that humans would rather destroy nature than experience it first-hand. In 'Lines Written in Early Spring', the speaker "laments" "What man has made of man", suggesting that he finds human behaviour upsetting and, unlike nature, humans cannot live in harmony. Although it is not clear what behaviour has upset the speaker, it could be the negative impact of the Industrial Revolution and the issues it caused for the environment.

AO3 — relate the poems to the context

- Although the poems were written over 200 years apart, both poets explore the beauty of nature, and suggest that spending time in nature can help to calm and soothe. This suggests that protecting and respecting nature is a universal theme in poetry.

This answer should be marked in accordance with the levels-based mark scheme on page 134.

Make sure your answer to this question is in paragraphs and full sentences. Bullet points have been used in this example answer to suggest some information you could include.

We've included some quotes from *Lines Written in Early Spring* (**page 10**) in this sample answer, but direct quotes from the comparison poem aren't essential; you can use paraphrased examples or summaries to demonstrate your understanding.

A PORTABLE PARADISE — ROGER ROBINSON

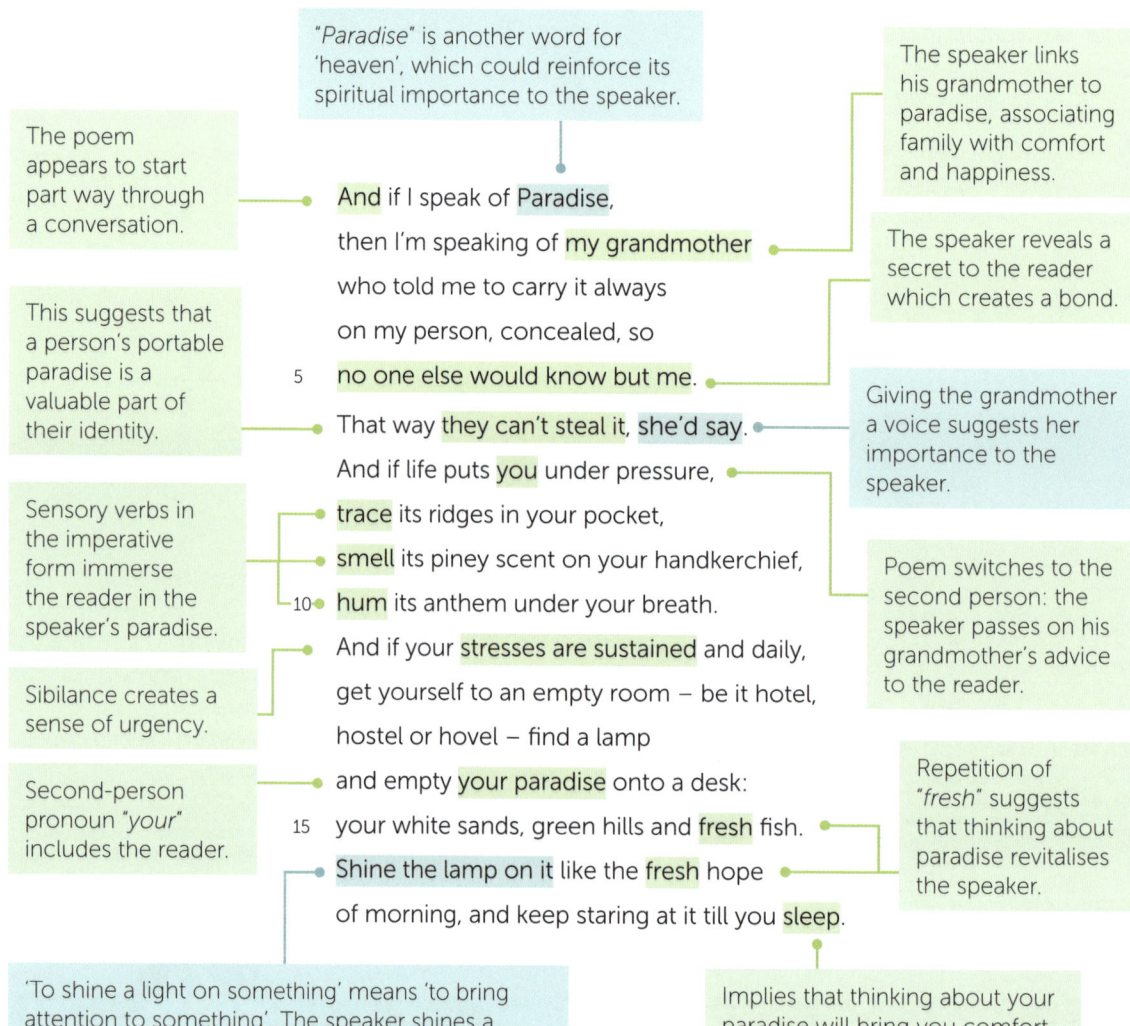

And if I speak of Paradise,
then I'm speaking of my grandmother
who told me to carry it always
on my person, concealed, so
5   no one else would know but me.
That way they can't steal it, she'd say.
And if life puts you under pressure,
trace its ridges in your pocket,
smell its piney scent on your handkerchief,
10   hum its anthem under your breath.
And if your stresses are sustained and daily,
get yourself to an empty room – be it hotel,
hostel or hovel – find a lamp
and empty your paradise onto a desk:
15   your white sands, green hills and fresh fish.
Shine the lamp on it like the fresh hope
of morning, and keep staring at it till you sleep.

Annotations:
- "*Paradise*" is another word for 'heaven', which could reinforce its spiritual importance to the speaker.
- The speaker links his grandmother to paradise, associating family with comfort and happiness.
- The poem appears to start part way through a conversation.
- The speaker reveals a secret to the reader which creates a bond.
- This suggests that a person's portable paradise is a valuable part of their identity.
- Giving the grandmother a voice suggests her importance to the speaker.
- Sensory verbs in the imperative form immerse the reader in the speaker's paradise.
- Poem switches to the second person: the speaker passes on his grandmother's advice to the reader.
- Sibilance creates a sense of urgency.
- Second-person pronoun "*your*" includes the reader.
- Repetition of "*fresh*" suggests that thinking about paradise revitalises the speaker.
- 'To shine a light on something' means 'to bring attention to something'. The speaker shines a light on his paradise, which could represent the importance of staying connected to your heritage.
- Implies that thinking about your paradise will bring you comfort.

Roger Robinson

Roger Robinson (b. 1967) is a British poet. He was born in London to Trinidadian parents. After he was born, he and his parents moved back to Trinidad. Robinson returned to England when he was nineteen and spent time living with his grandmother. *A Portable Paradise* was published in 2019.

Comment: *A Portable Paradise* could be interpreted as an **autobiographical** poem since it refers to the speaker's grandmother, and hints that his "*Paradise*" could be memories of his childhood in Trinidad (see **below**).

Roger Robinson

Summary of the poem

The speaker passes on advice that his grandmother gave him about using your imagination to create a paradise in your mind that you can carry around with you. The speaker suggests that our paradises are valuable, and must be protected from people who might try to steal them. The speaker suggests that everyone can have their own paradise to bring them comfort and escape from the stresses of everyday life.

Context and references

Trinidad and Tobago

Trinidad and Tobago is a dual-island nation which lies off the coast of Venezuela.

Comment: The speaker describes his paradise as having "*white sands, green hills and fresh fish*". The poet could be drawing on his own memories of Trinidad.

Maracas Bay, Trinidad

GCSE English Literature **Poetry Anthology | Worlds and Lives**

Themes

Identity
The speaker links paradise to his "*grandmother*", and the description of his paradise shares similarities with the poet's childhood home of Trinidad. This reinforces the importance of family and place to a person's identity.

Loneliness
The speaker struggles with the "*stresses*" of everyday life, but he finds comfort in his imagination rather than spending time with family and friends. This suggests he feels isolated.

Nature
The speaker's paradise has "*white sands*" and "*green hills*". This suggests that the speaker values the peace and beauty of nature.

Oppression
The speaker feels threatened by people who are trying to steal his paradise. This could reflect the discrimination the poet feels because of his Trinidadian heritage, and the pressure to suppress his cultural identity in order to 'fit in'.

Form and structure

A Portable Paradise shares features with a **monologue** (when a person speaks their thoughts out loud). The poem is written as a single stanza which suggests that it is the speaker's uninterrupted stream of consciousness. It is also written in **free verse** and the lines are frequently **enjambed** which more closely resembles natural speech.

Comment: The speaker may have used irregular line lengths with no set rhythm or rhyme scheme to convey how unpredictable life can be. This reinforces the importance of having a portable paradise to escape to.

This poem begins with "*And*", which suggests that the poem starts mid-way through a sentence, and draws the reader into the conversation.

Comment: The poem's conversational features create a sense of informality and closeness between the speaker and the reader, as if the speaker is talking to a friend.

The poem begins in the **first person**, which is typical of monologues, and makes the poem seem more personal. However, the speaker shifts to the **second person** from line 7. This directly addresses the reader, and reinforces the connection between the speaker and reader.

Comment: The speaker passes on advice he received from his grandmother. Many people have a very close relationship with their grandparents, so the reader may feel honoured that the speaker is willing to share this personal advice with them.

Tone

The poem has a reassuring tone. The speaker appears to be talking to someone who is also struggling with the "*pressure*" and "*stresses*" of life. The speaker provides the reader with advice on how to help them cope, and the poem ends with light imagery which creates a sense of hope.

Language

Representation of the speaker's paradise

Valuable

The speaker keeps his paradise "*concealed*" so that people cannot "*steal*" it. This implies that his paradise is precious, and he must keep it safe.

Comment: Although the speaker wants to keep his paradise hidden, he tells the reader about it. This creates a bond between the speaker and the reader, as if they are sharing a secret.

Inherited

The speaker's "*grandmother*" told him about portable paradises. This links paradise to a person's family and heritage.

Comment: The speaker gives his grandmother a voice in the poem ("*That way they can't steal it, she'd say*"), which reflects her importance to, and influence on, the speaker.

Comforting

The speaker's paradise allows him to escape the "*pressure*" and "*stresses*" of life, and he stares at it until he falls asleep. This suggests he finds his paradise comforting and soothing.

Attainable

The speaker suggests a portable paradise is accessible to anyone, whether they live in a "*hotel, / hostel or hovel*". He recognises that everyone may need a place to escape to, regardless of their social status.

Comment: The speaker uses the phrase "*your paradise*" which includes the reader and encourages them to think of their own paradise.

Natural

The speaker's description of paradise includes "*white sands*" and "*green hills*".

Comment: The speaker's version of paradise emphasises the importance of connecting with nature to escape the stress of daily life.

Language continued

Sensory language

The speaker uses **sensory language** to create a clear image of his paradise for the reader. The speaker allows the reader to imagine his version of paradise, something that is very personal to him. This creates intimacy between the reader and the speaker.

 The speaker can "*hum its anthem*".

 The speaker can taste "*fresh fish*".

 The speaker can "*trace its ridges*".

 The speaker can "*smell its piney scent*".

 The speaker can see "*white sands*".

Language of difficulty

The speaker implies that his paradise is at risk from an unnamed threat: "*they*" might "*steal it*". This suggests that the speaker is wary of the people around him.

Comment: This wariness implies the speaker feels threatened in his community, which reflects how immigrants often struggle with feelings of acceptance and belonging.

The lines "*get yourself to an empty room – be it hotel, / hostel or hovel – find a lamp*" use **caesura**. This creates a disjointed rhythm which implies a sense of urgency. This is reinforced by the **alliteration** of the 'h' sound which gives the phrase a breathless quality, which suggests that the speaker needs to be transported to his paradise immediately.

The speaker suggests that his life is difficult and that he needs his portable paradise to escape from his troubles. The speaker suggests that life can put you "*under pressure*" and that "*stresses are sustained and daily*".

Comment: Sibilance emphasises the phrase "*stresses are sustained*" which reinforces how gruelling life can be.

Language continued

Language of solitude and privacy

The speaker uses language associated with solitude and privacy. This could reflect how he feels disconnected from the world around him.

- He keeps his paradise private so that "*no one else would know but me*".
- He goes to an "*empty room*" to be alone with his paradise.
- His description of paradise doesn't include people, which could suggest he is happiest when he is by himself.

Comment: The poem's emphasis on solitude could also suggest that readers shouldn't rely on other people to help them find happiness.

Language of hope

The poem ends with a description of light imagery, including "*Shine the lamp*" and "*morning*". Light is often associated with hope, so ending the poem with these images leaves the reader with a sense of optimism.

Comment: The word "*fresh*" is repeated in the final lines of the poem. This implies that the speaker's paradise reinvigorates and revives him.

Command words

The speaker uses **imperative verbs** to command the reader, for example: "*trace*", "*smell*", "*hum*", "*get*", "*find*", "*Shine*" and "*keep*". This gives the reader clear instructions so that they can access their own portable paradise.

Comment: The imperatives also create a sense of urgency which reflects the importance of a portable paradise to the speaker.

COMPARING *A PORTABLE PARADISE*

Here's how *A Portable Paradise* could be compared to other poems.

> Remember, you can compare *A Portable Paradise* with any poem from the anthology as long as your response is supported with examples. The following examples suggest ways to compare the poems, but they are not complete answers.

Sense of threat

The speaker in *A Portable Paradise* feels threatened. The speaker describes how he has to keep his paradise "*concealed*" from people who might try to steal it. The people who threaten to steal the paradise are unnamed, and only referred to as "*they*". Using the third person pronoun suggests that the threat could be anyone, anywhere. This may represent how the speaker feels vulnerable as an ethnic minority, and the people who are trying to steal his "*paradise*" represent those who want him to suppress his culture and heritage to 'fit in' with the people around him.

Similarly, *Thirteen* (**page 122**) also explores the experiences of a speaker who feels threatened. However, the threat in this poem is more clear-cut: racism in the police force. The speaker describes being "*cornered*" by a police officer, which implies that the officer is trying to intimidate him, and reinforces the power imbalance between the speaker and the police. The speaker feels so threatened by the police that "*fear condenses*" on his lips: the speaker is sweating because he is terrified of what the police may do to him, even though he is innocent of any wrongdoing.

Longing for home

A Portable Paradise was written by Roger Robinson, who was born to Trinidadian parents and spent a significant part of his childhood in Trinidad, before moving to England. The paradise that the speaker describes with "*white sand*" and "*green hills*" shares some similarities with the landscape of Trinidad, which suggests that he longs to return. The speaker thinks about Trinidad to escape the "*stresses*" of daily life, which suggests that Trinidad is a place of comfort and security for the speaker.

Similarly, *Name Journeys* (see **pages 50–51**) was written by Raman Mundair, who was born in India, but moved to England as a child. The poem reinforces the speaker's love for her home country. For example, the speaker feels an affinity with the Hindu deity, Sita, and describes them as "*spiritual sari-sisters*". The word "*sister*" emphasises the connection she feels to her culture, and the importance of heritage and family to her identity. The speaker uses the comforting verbs "*entwined*" and "*swathe*" to describe being wrapped in Sita's sari, which suggests that thinking about India brings her reassurance.

Compare how poets present ideas about the natural world in *A Portable Paradise* and in **one** other poem from Worlds and Lives. [30 marks]

Your answer may include:

AO1 — show understanding of the poems

- Both 'A Portable Paradise' and 'Shall earth no more inspire thee' focus on individuals who feel lonely and isolated. They are both encouraged to find comfort and reassurance from the natural world.

AO2 — show understanding of the poets' language choices

- Both 'A Portable Paradise' and 'Shall earth no more inspire thee' compare the natural world to heaven on earth. The speaker in 'A Portable Paradise' describes his version of "paradise", and 'paradise' is another word for 'heaven'. The speaker's "paradise" includes descriptions of nature, such as "white sands" and "green hills". Similarly, in 'Shall earth no more inspire thee', the speaker includes descriptions of sunsets and mountain breezes, commenting "Yet none would ask a heaven / More like this earth than thine", suggesting that a version of heaven can be found in nature.

- The speakers in 'A Portable Paradise' and 'Shall earth no more inspire thee' both suggest that nature has the power to comfort and reassure. In 'A Portable Paradise', the speaker uses thoughts of nature to bring him comfort from the "pressure" and "stresses" of everyday life. Focusing on "white sands" and "green hills" allows him to "sleep". Similarly, the speaker in 'Shall earth no more inspire thee', suggests that the listener suffers from "dark" thoughts, implying that they are unhappy. The speaker comforts the listener by telling them that nature can "drive thy griefs away".

- Both poems use imperative verbs to urge the reader to connect with nature. The speaker in 'A Portable Paradise' uses the sensory verbs "trace", "smell" and "hum" to encourage the reader to imagine their own version of paradise. The speaker in 'Shall earth no more inspire thee' uses imperative verbs to encourage the listener to spend time in nature, such as "Come", "dwell" and "Return".

AO3 — relate the poems to the context

- It's likely that both poets were inspired by the places around them. Robinson's version of paradise shares similarities with his childhood home of Trinidad. Similarly, Brontë spent a lot of time on the Yorkshire moors, so her representation of nature was likely influenced by English moorland.

This answer should be marked in accordance with the levels-based mark scheme on page 134.

Make sure your answer to this question is in paragraphs and full sentences. Bullet points have been used in this example answer to suggest some information you could include.

We've included some quotes from *Shall earth no more inspire thee* (**pages 26–27**) in this sample answer, but direct quotes from the comparison poem aren't essential; you can use paraphrased examples or summaries to demonstrate your understanding.

LIKE AN HEIRESS — GRACE NICHOLS

"*jewels*" extends the imagery of the speaker inheriting something valuable.

The simile suggests the speaker is due to inherit something valuable, which could refer to the poet's Guyanese heritage.

The speaker feels a connection to the Atlantic Ocean, and it reminds her of her childhood ("*small-days*").

"*But*" introduces a volta (turning point).

List of three reinforces the scale of the pollution on the beach.

The speaker personifies the ocean and sympathises with how it has been treated.

Suggests the speaker finds comfort in her hotel room rather than her home country, which hints that she feels disconnected from Guyana.

Like an heiress, drawn to the light of her
eye-catching jewels, Atlantic draws me
to the mirror of my oceanic small-days.
But the beach is deserted except for a lone
5   wave of rubbish against the seawall -
used car tyres, plastic bottles, styrofoam cups
rightly tossed back by an ocean's moodswings.
Undisturbed, not even by a sea bird,
I stand under the sun's burning treasury
10 gazing out at the far-out gleam of Atlantic
before heading back like a tourist
to the sanctuary of my hotel room
to dwell in the air-conditioned coolness
on the quickening years and fate of our planet.

This pause could reflect the speaker's shock at what she sees.

Implies that the environmental damage has affected wildlife as well as the ocean.

This simile contrasts with "*like an heiress*" and suggests she no longer belongs.

The poem ends with a sense of hopelessness for the future of the planet. The phrase "*quickening years*" implies humans are running out of time to solve the climate crisis.

The speaker uses the plural pronoun to include the reader in her concern.

Contrasts with the "*burning*" sun.

Grace Nichols

Grace Nichols (b 1950) was born in British Guiana (see **below**), and spent part of her childhood in a small coastal town, before moving to the capital, Georgetown. She moved to Britain in 1977. *Like an Heiress* was published in 2020 and was inspired by a trip Nichols took to Guyana.

Grace Nichols

Summary of the poem

The speaker visits a beach on the Atlantic where she spent her childhood. The beach is empty apart from a large amount of rubbish that has been washed up on the shore. The speaker watches the ocean for a moment, then goes back to her hotel room feeling a sense of despair for the future of the planet.

Context and references

Guyana

Guyana is a country in the northern part of South America which is bordered by the Atlantic Ocean. Between 1831-1966, Guyana was controlled by Britain and was known as British Guiana. When the nation regained its independence in 1966, it became Guyana.

Tourism

Comment: The speaker compares herself to a *"tourist"*. She may feel as though tourism is partly responsible for the environmental damage she sees in Guyana.

Some tourism contributes to environmental damage, as long-haul flights emit carbon emissions which damage the atmosphere.

Comment: The sun is described as *"burning"* which could hint at the threat of global warming.

Tourism can also negatively impact developing nations, such as Guyana, as these countries don't have the infrastructure to deal with an influx of tourists. This can lead to vital local services, such as waste management, being overwhelmed, creating a build up of rubbish. A recent study found that Guyana ranks 6th in the world for ocean plastic pollution.

Rubbish washed up on a beach

GCSE English Literature Poetry Anthology | Worlds and Lives

Themes

Nature
Nature is presented as valuable and beautiful. The Atlantic Ocean is compared to "*eye-catching jewels*" and the sun is a "*treasury*".

Identity
The speaker is initially excited to return to a place where she spent her childhood, suggesting that it is important to her identity.

Environmental damage
The speaker is shocked to see a "*wave of rubbish*" on the beach, showing humankind's negative impact on the environment.

Belonging
The speaker feels like a "*tourist*" in a place she spent time as a child. This suggests she doesn't feel as though she belongs there anymore.

Loneliness
Words such as "*deserted*", "*lone*" and "*Undisturbed*" suggest that humankind has abandoned nature and left it to suffer alone.

Form and structure

Like an Heiress consists of a single stanza made up of fourteen lines. This links the poem's form to a **sonnet** (see **page 20**).

Comment: Sonnets were usually reserved for love poetry. Nichols may have used this form to express the love she feels towards her native Guyana.

However, *Like an Heiress* is written in **free verse**, so it does not use the traditional rhythm or rhyme scheme typically found in sonnets. The speaker may have rejected these conventions to reinforce the uneasy tone of the poem.

The poem begins with an upbeat tone as the speaker feels like an "*heiress*" when returns to a place she spent time as a child. However, the **volta**, signalled by "*But*" on line 4 introduces the speaker's disappointment at seeing the beach covered with rubbish.

Comment: The dash at the end of line 5 could reflect the speaker's shock as she looks at the rubbish piled up on the beach.

The poem is written in the **first person**, which matches the intimate and personal nature of this autobiographical poem. However, in the final line, the speaker uses the plural pronoun "*our*" in the phrase "*fate of our planet*" which includes the reader in the concern she feels for Earth. This emphasises how environmental damage is a problem we must solve collectively.

Tone

Like an Heiress begins with an excited tone. The speaker is *"drawn"* to the beauty of the Atlantic Ocean, and it reminds her of her childhood.

The poem then shifts to a reflective tone, as the speaker stands by the shore *"gazing out"* at the ocean, thinking about the rubbish piled on the beach.

The poem ends with a despondent tone as the speaker is faced with the reality of humankind's negative impact on nature.

Language

Representation of the speaker

The poem opens with the **simile** *"Like an heiress"* to describe the speaker returning to a place she spent time as a child. Since the poem is autobiographical, it describes Nichols returning to her home country of Guyana. The word *"heiress"* implies that the speaker will inherit something precious and valuable, reinforcing the value of her Guyanese heritage. This is reinforced by the description of the *"eye-catching jewels"* of the Atlantic, which could refer to the light sparkling on the ocean, like gems sparkling in sunlight.

The speaker is *"drawn"* to the ocean, which suggests she feels a strong connection to the Atlantic that is almost subconscious.

However, after the speaker sees the rubbish on the beach, she uses the **simile** *"like a tourist"*, which contrasts with the title *Like an Heiress*. The change from *"heiress"* to *"tourist"* implies that she no longer feels a connection to Guyana, and she is a stranger in her own country. This might reflect her disappointment that the Guyanese people haven't taken care of their beaches, or it may represent her shame that her own environmental impact has negatively affected her home country, and that she no longer deserves to be an *"heiress"*.

The speaker reflects on her experiences. She is described as *"gazing out"* at the ocean, and she returns to her hotel to *"dwell"*. These verbs suggest she cannot stop thinking about the rubbish on the beach and has been deeply affected by what she has seen.

The speaker returns to her *"air-conditioned"* hotel room to escape the sight of the pollution and the heat of the sun. This could suggest that the speaker feels disconnected from nature, but it also suggests that she is part of the problem, as air conditioning units contain greenhouse gases and consume a lot of energy, which both contribute to global warming.

> **Comment:** The speaker refers to her hotel as a *"sanctuary"*. This suggests she feels more comfortable in her hotel room than she does outside in Guyana. This adds to the speaker's sense of disconnection from her home country.

The speaker's trip to the beach leaves her feeling despondent, and she reflects on the *"fate"* of the planet.

Language continued

Representation of nature

Ocean: The ocean is presented as beautiful and precious as the speaker is *"drawn to the light of her / eye-catching jewels"*. The image of the ocean sparkling is repeated in the phrase *"far-out gleam"*. However, *"far-out"* suggests that the beauty of the ocean is diminishing because of the pollution.

Comment: The ocean is **personified** as having *"moodswings"*, which suggests that it is annoyed by humankind's lack of respect. The ocean has also *"tossed back"* the rubbish that has ended up in the sea which suggests it is trying to fight back.

Beach: The beach is *"deserted"* suggesting that people don't want to go there because it is dirty and piled with a *"lone / wave of rubbish"*.

Birds: The pile of rubbish is *"Undisturbed"* by sea birds. Most sea birds, such as gulls, are scavengers, but even they want no part in humankind's destruction of the environment.

Comment: The words *"deserted"*, *"lone"* and *"Undisturbed"* contribute to a feeling of isolation, and suggest that humankind is not prepared to help nature.

Sun: The speaker stands *"under the sun's burning treasury"*. The word *"burning"* suggests that the sun is damaging, and could hint at the issue of global warming.

Comment: The word *"treasury"* links back to the idea of the speaker being an *"heiress"*. However, *"burning"* suggests that the speaker's inheritance is painful.

The planet: The speaker ends the poem by describing the *"quickening years and fate of our planet"*. This suggests humans are running out of time to reverse environmental damage. This ends the poem with a pessimistic tone.

Language continued

Representation of the rubbish

The pile of rubbish is introduced as a **triplet** (list of three): "*used car tyres, plastic bottles, styrofoam cups*". Listing the items emphasises the amount of the pollution on the beach, creating a devastating image.

> **Comment:** The rubbish is described as a "*wave*". This hints that pollution is beginning to overwhelm nature.

Included in the rubbish are "*plastic bottles, styrofoam cups*", both single-use items used for convenience. This highlights humankind's wasteful nature which jeopardises the planet and our own future.

COMPARING *LIKE AN HEIRESS*

Here's how *Like an Heiress* could be compared to other poems.

> Remember, you can compare *Like an Heiress* with any poem from the anthology as long as your response is supported with examples. The following examples suggest ways to compare the poems, but they are not complete answers.

Sonnet form

Like an Heiress shares some similarities with a sonnet form. It is made up of fourteen lines, and introduces a volta on line 4 ("*But*"). However, *Like an Heiress* is written in free verse so it doesn't use the traditional rhythm or rhyme scheme of sonnets. Sonnets are typically used for love poetry, so the speaker may have chosen this form to reflect the love she feels towards her childhood home. However, the lack of rhythm and rhyme scheme could suggest the speaker's sadness and disappointment towards the environmental damage she witnesses.

England in 1819 (see **page 18**) is also loosely based on a sonnet. Although it doesn't perfectly match either a Shakespearian or Petrarchan sonnet, it more closely follows the sonnet conventions than *Like an Heiress*, as it has a sestet with an ABABAB rhyme scheme, a quatrain with a CDCD rhyme scheme and ends with two pairs of couplets. The sonnet form could suggest the speaker's love for England, but the unexpected rhyme scheme could reflect his feelings of disconnection from the powerful institutions which govern England.

Human impact on the environment

Like an Heiress explores humankind's negative impact on the environment, specifically rubbish which ends up in the ocean. The speaker personifies the ocean, describing how it "*rightly*" tosses this rubbish back on to the shore which suggests that the speaker sympathises with the ocean. The speaker also personifies the ocean as having "*moodswings*", which suggests that the ocean is angry at how it is treated by humankind. Personifying the ocean makes humankind's environmental damage seem even worse because the speaker implies humans are harming a living thing with emotions and feelings.

With Birds You're Never Lonely (see **pages 98–99**) also considers humankind's impact on the environment. The speaker reflects on a book about trees, and hints that it is ironic how humankind cuts down trees to make books about trees. This reminds the reader of the damage that humans do the environment, and emphasises how humankind is becoming disconnected from nature. This is reinforced with the image of the "*grey tree*" in London. The colour grey is associated with weakness and misery, suggesting that urbanisation has negatively impacted the trees in London. This contrasts with the sturdy "*brown and green*" trees in the New Zealand forest, suggesting that they thrive when they are far away from human interference.

Compare how poets present ideas about nature in *Like an Heiress* and in **one** other poem from Worlds and Lives. [30 marks]

Your answer may include:

AO1 — show understanding of the poems

- *Both 'Like an Heiress' and 'In a London Drawingroom' explore the human impact on nature, and criticise the negative impact that pollution has had on the environment.*

AO2 — show understanding of the poets' language choices

- *Both speakers suggest that nature is beautiful and valuable. In 'Like an Heiress', the speaker compares the Atlantic Ocean to "eye-catching jewels", suggesting that it is beautiful and precious. Similarly, 'In a London Drawingroom' the speaker describes the sun's "golden rays". The word "golden" has connotations of treasure, hinting that sunlight is beautiful and valuable.*

- *Both poems explore the environmental damage caused by humans. In 'Like an Heiress', the speaker uses a triplet to list the "car tyres, plastic bottles, styrofoam cups" which emphasises the extent of the waste on the beach. This is reinforced by the speaker describing the rubbish as a "wave" which implies that pollution is beginning to overwhelm the ocean. Similarly, the speaker in 'In a London Drawingroom' describes how the sky is "yellowed by the smoke". This suggests that the thick air pollution caused by factories turns the sky an unnatural, unpleasant colour. The speaker suggests that the pollution is inescapable with descriptions of "solid fog", "all is shadow" and "thickest canvass". This suggests the pollution is dense and widespread.*

- *Both speakers are upset by the pollution, which causes them to feel disconnected from their surroundings. In 'Like an Heiress', the speaker uses a simile "like a tourist" which suggests that she feels like a stranger in the country that she grew up in. This phrase could also be a criticism of long-haul tourism, and the negative impact it has on the environment. Similarly, the speaker in 'In a London Drawingroom' describes London as a "prison-house". This suggests she feels confined by her surroundings, and as though she is being punished.*

AO3 — relate the poems to the context

- *Both poems reflect on environmental damage, but the cause of the damage is different. 'Like an Heiress' could be commenting on the negative impact that tourism is having on developing countries, such as Guyana, suggesting that long-haul flights and unsustainable tourism is contributing to environmental damage. On the other hand, 'In a London Drawingroom', criticises the negative impact of the Industrial Revolution on London in the 19th century.*

This answer should be marked in accordance with the levels-based mark scheme on page 134.

Make sure your answer to this question is in paragraphs and full sentences. Bullet points have been used in this example answer to suggest some information you could include.

We've included some quotes from *In a London Drawingroom* (**page 34**) in this sample answer, but direct quotes from the comparison poem aren't essential; you can use paraphrased examples or summaries to demonstrate your understanding.

THIRTEEN — CALEB FEMI

Second person pronoun directly addresses the reader.

The poem starts in media res which reinforces the shock felt by the speaker.

"*cornered***" suggests the officers made the speaker feel vulnerable.**

You will be four minutes from home
when you are cornered by an officer
who will tell you of a robbery, forty
minutes ago in the area. *You fit*
5 *the description of a man?* — You'll laugh.
Thirteen, you'll tell him: you're thirteen.

Direct speech is signaled using italics.

Repetition of "*thirteen*" reinforces the speaker's youth, and contrasts with the word "*man*".

You'll be patted on the shoulder, then, by another fed
whose face takes you back to Gloucester Primary School,
a Wednesday assembly about *being little stars.*
10 This same officer had an horizon in the east
of his smile when he told your class that
you were all supernovas,
the biggest and brightest stars.

The speaker recalls a memory from a few years prior.

The police officer compared the children to "*stars*" suggesting they had a bright future. This hints at the hypocrisy of the officer.

You will show the warmth of your teeth
15 praying he remembers the heat of your supernova;
he will see you powerless — plump.
You will watch the two men cast lots for your organs.

The speaker smiles to show he is not a threat.

This reinforces the speaker's youth and how unlike a "*man*" he is.

The speaker can only "*watch*" which emphasises his powerlessness.

Don't you remember me? you will ask.
You gave a talk at my primary school.
20 While fear condenses on your lips,
you will remember that Wednesday, after the assembly,
your teacher speaking more about supernovas:
how they are, in fact, dying stars
on the verge of becoming black holes.

This metaphor describes the speaker beginning to sweat which reinforces his fear and nervousness. The speaker doesn't feel safe around the police officers because he recognises he is being discriminated against.

"*black holes*" suggests the speaker's despair. The word "*black*" hints at the speaker's skin colour.

? fed — a police officer

Caleb Femi

Caleb Femi (b. 1990) was born in Nigeria but moved to London when he was seven. *Thirteen* is taken from Femi's collection *Poor*, published in 2020, which explores themes including discrimination.

Comment: The poem refers to "*Gloucester Primary School*". This is a real primary school in Peckham, London where Femi grew up. This suggests that elements of the poem are **autobiographical**.

Caleb Femi

Summary of the poem

The speaker recalls being stopped by police officers on his way home from school when he was 13. The police officers tell him that he matches the description of a man who committed a robbery in the area. The speaker recognises one of the police officers who gave a talk at his primary school and told the pupils that they were "*supernovas*". The speaker asks the police officer if he remembers him, and recalls that supernovas are dying stars.

Comment: Although it is never stated, it is assumed that the speaker is other than white.

Context and references

Police discrimination and brutality

White people in Britain are less likely to experience discrimination from the police than people of other ethnicities, particularly young, black males. Examples of discrimination can include:

- being falsely accused of crimes with little or no evidence.
- being apprehended with disproportionate levels of force.
- police officers not being adequately punished for discriminatory behaviour.

People protesting police brutality in London, 2020.

This discrimination has led to some people becoming mistrustful towards law enforcement: they do not believe the police will treat them fairly.

Around the time Femi published *Thirteen*, an unarmed black man in America called George Floyd was murdered by white police officers as they detained him for supposedly using a fake $20 bill. This event contributed to the rise of the **Black Lives Matter** movement which brought greater attention to police brutality in America and elsewhere around the world.

Themes

Prejudice

It is implied that the speaker is stopped by police because he is a black male.

Oppression

The speaker doesn't attempt to stand up to the police officers. This could be because people who are other than white are often treated more severely than white people for non-compliance.

Form and structure

Thirteen is a **narrative poem** written in the **second person**. Using the second person directly addresses the reader and makes them feel as though they are experiencing the discrimination first-hand. This helps the reader to empathise with the speaker.

The poem is written in the **future tense**, using the modal verb "*will*". This reinforces the idea that discrimination is inevitable for many people.

The poem is written in **free verse** and uses **enjambment**. This more closely matches everyday speech, and creates a conversational tone which helps to establish intimacy with the reader. The enjambment in the first stanza helps to increase the pace, which reflects the speaker's panic.

Comment: The speaker uses **caesura** in lines 5-6 to create a disjointed rhythm. This reinforces the speaker's disbelief that he has been mistaken for a "*man*".

The poem begins **in media res** (in the middle of the action). This reflects the speaker's surprise and confusion at being apprehended by the police.

The poem is made up of four stanzas of unequal length. This irregular structure could match the unpredictability of the speaker's situation.

The poem ends without the reader finding out what happens to the speaker. This creates a sense of uncertainty which reflects the unease felt by some people around law enforcement.

Comment: The poem ends with a pessimistic tone, implying that some children are denied the chance of a bright future because of the discrimination they face.

Tone

The poem has an uneasy tone as it reinforces the power imbalance between the police officers and the speaker. The speaker's fear suggests that the situation could escalate.

The poem has an ironic tone, and it highlights the hypocrisy of the police officer. When the speaker is at primary school, the officer thinks he is a "*star*" which implies the officer believes he has the potential to do great things. Only a few years later, the same officer assumes he is a criminal.

The poem ends with a sense of hopelessness. The speaker likens himself and other children to "*dying stars / on the verge of becoming black holes*". This reinforces how experience of prejudice can negatively impact a person's feelings of self-worth.

Language

Language of youth and powerlessness

In the first stanza, the speaker is walking home when he is apprehended by the officers. This establishes that he isn't behaving in a suspicious way when he is accused of the robbery. This reinforces the injustice of the accusations and implies that the speaker is only suspected by the police because he is a black male.

> **Comment:** The speaker is only "*four minutes*" from home. This suggests police discrimination can happen anywhere, even close to the safety of your home.

The speaker repeats the word "*thirteen*" which reinforces the speaker's youth, and how absurd it is that he has been mistaken for a "*man*". This also reminds readers how so many people in Britain can experience police discrimination from a young age.

> **Comment:** The speaker laughs when he is first apprehended by the police. This suggests he thinks that he has been stopped for a joke. However, his amusement turns to "*fear*" when he realises that it is not a joke, and he suspects he will not be treated fairly by the police.

The speaker shows "*the warmth of [his] teeth*". This suggests he smiles at the officer to prove he is not a threat.

> Many people from marginalised communities who are accused of breaking the law will choose not to stand up for themselves because they do not want to appear aggressive and suffer retaliation.

The speaker describes himself as "*powerless - plump*" which implies he looks unthreatening and youthful, but it also highlights how ridiculous it is that he looks like a "*man*".

> **Comment:** The word "*plump*" also suggests that the officers are predators who see him as prey. This links to the image of them fighting over his "*organs*" (see **page 126**).

The speaker is described as "*praying*" and can only "*watch*" as the officers decide his fate. This reinforces his powerlessness.

The speaker describes how "*fear condenses*" on his lips. This **metaphor** describes how the speaker begins to sweat, highlighting his fear and nervousness.

GCSE English Literature **Poetry Anthology | Worlds and Lives**

Language continued

Representation of the police officers

Intimidating

The police officers "*cornered*" the speaker. This suggests that they are trying to intimidate him and highlights the power imbalance between the adult police officers and the speaker.

Hypocritical

As a child, the police officer thinks the speaker is a "*supernova*" with a bright future ahead of him. However, when he is a teenager, the police officer assumes the speaker is a thief.

Heartless

The officers "*cast lots*" for the speaker's "*organs*". 'Casting lots' describes making a decision on a random outcome: for example, rolling dice or flipping a coin. This phrase suggests that the officers use a trivial method to determine the speaker's fate, highlighting his unimportance to them.

Comment: The metaphorical image of the officers deciding who gets the speaker's "*organs*" also presents them as brutal and savage, suggesting that they see him as prey.

Comment: For people from non-marginalised communities, police officers are often presented as brave people who protect law-abiding citizens from criminals, so the representation of the officers in the poem may shock some readers.

Language continued

Language associated with stars

When the police officer gives a talk at the speaker's primary school, he calls the pupils "*little stars*" and "*supernovas*": the officer believes the pupils are bright and full of potential.

However, in the final stanza, the speaker extends this **metaphor** and explains that supernovas are "*dying stars / on the verge of becoming black holes*". The word "*dying*" reinforces how the speaker feels his potential has been ended by the discrimination he will face. The phrase "*black hole*" suggests that discrimination can make people feel empty and worthless.

COMPARING THIRTEEN

Here's how *Thirteen* could be compared to other poems.

> Remember, you can compare *Thirteen* with any poem from the anthology as long as your response is supported with examples. The following examples suggest ways to compare the poems, but they are not complete answers.

Prejudice

Thirteen explores a speaker's experience of racial prejudice when, aged 13, he is wrongly accused of a crime committed by a *"man"*. Although it is never explicitly stated, it is implied that the police apprehend the speaker because he is a young, black male, highlighting the issue of racial discrimination in the British police force. The speaker emphasises his youth throughout the poem, repeating that he is only *"thirteen"* and describing himself as *"powerless - plump"*. Presenting himself as child-like reinforces the power imbalance between the speaker and the police officers who stop him, as well as reminding readers that some people face discrimination from a very young age.

Name Journeys (see **pages 50–51**) examines the experiences of an Asian person living in Britain, and the prejudice she faces. The speaker immigrated from India to Manchester at a young age, and even though she has spent decades living in England, she describes how her voice is *"a mystery / in the Anglo echo chamber"*. This suggests that English people ignore minority voices, and would rather listen to 'white' perspectives. This implies that English people view 'white' opinions as more important than those of other ethnicities.

Hopelessness

Thirteen ends with a sense of hopelessness. As a child, the speaker is compared to *"supernovas, / the biggest and brightest stars"*. This suggests that he is full of potential and has a bright future ahead of him. However, as a teenager, he experiences police discrimination, and this changes his perception of supernovas, describing them as *"dying stars / on the verge of becoming black holes"*. The word *"dying"* implies that his potential is fading, and the phrase *"black holes"* could refer to feelings of anger and emptiness experienced by those who face discrimination on a regular basis. Ending the poem in this way suggests many children are denied a bright future because of prejudice.

Like an Heiress (see **page 114**) also leaves the reader with a feeling of hopelessness. This poem explores how humankind's disregard for the environment has ruined a beach which was of sentimental importance to the speaker. The experience causes the speaker to reflect on the *"quickening years and fate of our planet"*. The phrase *"quickening years"* implies that humans are running out of time to resolve the climate crisis.

Compare how poets present ideas about prejudice in *Thirteen* and in **one** other poem from Worlds and Lives.

[30 marks]

Your answer may include:

AO1 — show understanding of the poems

- Both 'Thirteen' and 'On an Afternoon Train...' explore experiences of prejudice. The speaker in 'Thirteen' faces the overt prejudice of police discrimination, while the speaker in 'On an Afternoon Train...' faces a subtler form of prejudice: racial ignorance.

AO2 — show understanding of the poets' language choices

- Both poems focus on a speaker who experiences prejudice during an interaction with someone else. In 'On an Afternoon Train...' the speaker has a conversation with an ignorant Quaker, and in 'Thirteen' the speaker suffers racial discrimination from the police. Both speakers use free verse, enjambment, and direct speech to present these conversations. This makes the events seem more realistic, and reflects the autobiographical nature of the poems highlighting how prejudice is a reality for many people in Britain.

- Both speakers remain polite when faced with prejudice. This could reflect how minorities often feel as though they can't call out discrimination because they may be putting themselves at risk. In 'Thirteen', the speaker smiles at the police officers showing the "warmth" of his teeth. This suggests he wants to appear friendly and unthreatening, even though he is being treated unfairly. In 'On an Afternoon Train...', the speaker patiently replies to the Quaker's ignorant questions, such as "What part of Africa is Jamaica?". The speaker is repeatedly described as being "thoughtful" which suggests he wants to carefully consider his responses.

- Both poems suggest that the speakers are negatively impacted by their experiences of prejudice. In 'Thirteen', the speaker initially is compared to a supernova, suggesting he is full of potential. However, as he grows up and is more aware of the prejudice he will face as an adult, he reflects that he is on the "verge" of becoming a "black hole". The image of a black hole implies that he feels angry and empty by the way he is treated by society. In 'On an Afternoon Train...', the Quaker's ignorant questions trigger a memory of the speaker's father's banana field. This suggests that he feels homesick, because he doesn't feel welcome in England.

AO3 — relate the poems to the context

- 'On an Afternoon Train...' explores attitudes towards minorities in 1955 following the influx of immigrants to England after the Second World War. This marked the start of multiculturalism in Britain, when there may have been a lot of curiosity towards people from different nationalities. However, 'Thirteen', which was written over 50 years later, suggests that racial discrimination still occurs in British society.

This answer should be marked in accordance with the levels-based mark scheme on page 134.

⭐ Make sure your answer to this question is in paragraphs and full sentences. Bullet points have been used in this example answer to suggest some information you could include.

We've included some quotes from *On an Afternoon Train...* **(pages 42–43)** in this sample answer, but direct quotes from the comparison poem aren't essential; you can use paraphrased examples to demonstrate your understanding.

OVERVIEW OF THEMES

Here's a summary of the themes across the cluster. Use it to help you quickly identify which poems share similar themes.

Poem	Oppression	Nature	Belonging	Prejudice	Migration	Identity	Spirituality & religion	Loneliness	Environmental damage
Lines Written in Early Spring	✓	✓	✓				✓		
England in 1819	✓								
Shall earth no more inspire thee		✓					✓	✓	
In a London Drawingroom		✓						✓	✓
On an Afternoon Train…			✓	✓	✓				
Name Journeys			✓	✓	✓		✓	✓	
pot			✓		✓	✓			
A Wider View			✓						✓
Homing			✓	✓		✓			
A century later	✓								
The Jewellery Maker	✓		✓			✓			
With Birds You're Never Lonely			✓					✓	✓
A Portable Paradise	✓	✓				✓		✓	
Like an Heiress		✓	✓			✓		✓	✓
Thirteen	✓			✓					

> ★ This isn't an exhaustive list of themes. Instead, it's a summary of some of the themes which are shared by two or more poems and are likely to be relevant to the exam question.

EXAMINATION PRACTICE

> **Instructions and information:**
> - We have provided three exam-style questions below. In the exam, you will only be given one question.
> - For realistic practice, find an unannotated version of the poem specified in the question, either from your anthology or online.
> - You should allow around 45 minutes to answer each question.
> - Write your answers on a separate sheet of paper using black ink.

1. Compare how poets present ideas about belonging in *Name Journeys* and **one** other poem from Worlds and Lives. [30 marks]

   You can choose any poem from the anthology, but the example answer uses In a London Drawingroom *for comparison.*

2. Compare how poets present ideas about place and identity in *Homing* and **one** other poem from Worlds and Lives. [30 marks]

   You can choose any poem from the anthology, but the example answer uses The Jewellery Maker *for comparison.*

3. Compare how poets present ideas about nature in *Like an Heiress* and **one** other poem from Worlds and Lives. [30 marks]

   You can choose any poem from the anthology, but the example answer uses Shall earth no more inspire thee *for comparison.*

EXAMINATION PRACTICE ANSWERS

These answers should only be used as a guide. They are not exhaustive, and there are lots of alternative points that could be made. Your answers may also be structured differently. Use the levels-based mark scheme on page 134 to help you self-mark your answers.

1. Both *Name Journeys* and *In a London Drawingroom* focus on speakers who feel as though they don't belong. Although they were written almost 150 years apart, both speakers present themselves as feeling lonely and disconnected from the world around them.

    It is likely that both poems are autobiographical and explore the experiences and feelings of the poet. *Name Journeys* was written by Raman Mundair who immigrated to Manchester from India when she was a child. *In a London Drawingroom* was written by George Eliot, who grew up in a rural area in Britain and moved to London later in life. Both poets suggest that they don't belong in the place they have moved to. In *Name Journeys*, the speaker comments that her name became a "*stumble*" in English mouths, meaning that English people found it difficult to say her name. This suggests that every time someone mispronounced her name, the speaker was reminded that she wasn't from England, and that she didn't belong. Similarly, *In a London Drawingroom*, the speaker comments that the carriages are "*closed*". This suggests that the speaker feels shut out from the people around her, and as though she is not welcome in London.

    Both poets use form to reinforce their feelings of disconnection. *Name Journeys* is based on a type of poetry called a ghazal. Ghazals typically explore ideas around the pain of separation, so this form could reflect the pain felt by the speaker at being separated from her home country of India. Typically, ghazals have a set rhyme, however, the poet subverts this convention, and uses free verse. The lack of rhyme scheme could reflect how she doesn't feel as though she belongs in England. *In a London Drawingroom* is written as a single, unbroken stanza. This dense block of text looks like a barrier, which could reflect how the speaker feels trapped in London. Like *Name Journeys*, the poet doesn't use a rhyme scheme. This could reflect how she doesn't feel as though she has integrated into London society.

    Both poems end with a sense of hopelessness, which suggests to the reader that the poets will continue to feel disconnected from the world around them. In *Name Journeys*, the speaker ends the poem with a criticism of the "*Anglo echo chamber*". This suggests that minority voices, such as her own, aren't listened to in British society, and without empathy and understanding, immigrants will continue to feel as though they do not belong. Similarly, in *In a London Drawingroom*, the speaker ends the poem by commenting that London feels like a "*prison-house*". This suggests that she feels as though she is trapped, and that living in London feels like a punishment. This ends the poem on a pessimistic note, and gives the reader little hope that the speaker will ever feel as though she belongs in London.

2. Both *Homing* and *The Jewellery Maker* explore ideas around inequality. In *Homing*, the speaker describes someone who was judged because of their Midlands accent, so they took elocution lessons to disguise the way they spoke. In *The Jewellery Maker*, the goldsmith makes beautiful pieces of jewellery, but his family is poor. This suggests that he isn't paid fairly by the people who buy his work. Despite highlighting experiences of inequality, both poems suggest the importance of being proud of your identity.

    Homing presents class prejudice which existed in 20th century Britain. The speaker describes someone who metaphorically hides their Midlands accent "*in a box*" with a "*rusted*" lock. This suggests that they were so ashamed of their accent, they repressed it for a very long time. In the past, the Midlands accent was associated with heavy industry, so it was judged as a 'working-class' accent, and speakers were thought to be poor and uneducated. People with a Midlands accent would take elocution lessons to hide the way they spoke, and avoid the stigma attached to the accent. In *The Jewellery Maker*, the speaker highlights the social inequality experienced by the jewellery maker and his family. The speaker compares the jewellery maker's wife with the women who buy his pieces. The wife wears "*a plain gold band*", implying that the jewellery maker could only afford a simple ring for his wife. However, his customers buy intricate jewellery decorated with "*flowers*" and "*butterflies*", which suggests that they can afford to buy ornate, luxury pieces. This suggests that even though the jewellery maker is highly skilled and works with precious metal, he is not paid well enough to afford beautiful jewellery for his wife.

    Despite facing inequality, both poems suggest the speakers are proud of their identities. The speaker in *Homing* is proud of the Midlands' industrial past, commenting that she wanted to "*lick the coal*" from Midlands' dialect words and "*swallow... the pits*". These phrases link the Midlands accent with its coal mining heritage, and the verbs "*swallow*" and "*lick*" suggest that the speaker wants this heritage to become a part of her. In *The Jewellery Maker*, the goldsmith sits "*straight-backed*", and this posture implies that he takes his work seriously. He also lays out his tools "*as neat as soldiers*", and this simile conveys the pride he takes in his work.

3. Both *Like an Heiress* and *Shall earth no more inspire thee* focus on disconnected relationships between humankind and the natural world. In *Like an Heiress*, humans have treated nature disrespectfully by polluting the ocean with rubbish. In *Shall earth no more inspire thee*, the subject is unhappy, and she has lost interest in the natural world. Both poems suggest that humans suffer when we do not live in harmony with nature.

Both poems present nature as beautiful. In *Like an Heiress*, the speaker compares the Atlantic Ocean to "*eye-catching jewels*", suggesting that the water is sparkling in the sunlight. Likening the ocean to "*jewels*", implies that nature is beautiful and precious. In *Shall earth no more inspire thee*, the speaker also highlights the beauty of nature, comparing it to "*heaven*". This suggests that nature is like a paradise on Earth, filled with beauty.

Despite presenting nature as beautiful, both poems focus on people who have become disconnected from nature. In *Like an Heiress*, the speaker despairs at the way that nature has been polluted by humans. When she sees the rubbish on the beach, the speaker returns to the "*sanctuary*" of her hotel room. This suggests that she finds her hotel room comforting, because she doesn't want to see the damage that humans have done to the beach, and she feels disconnected from the world around her. In *Shall earth no more inspire thee*, the subject could be suffering from depression, and has consequently lost interest in nature. The speaker describes how the subject suffers from "*dark*" thoughts and is overwhelmed by "*griefs*", and because of this, the speaker asks, "*Shall earth no more inspire thee*", suggesting that the speaker is no longer impressed by nature.

Both poems personify nature to reinforce it as powerful, living entity. Personification also allows the poems to comment on the relationships between nature and humankind. In *Like an Heiress*, the speaker describes how the ocean has "*moodswings*". This suggests that the ocean is angry at the way it has been treated by humans. The speaker also describes how the ocean has "*tossed back*" humankind's trash, suggesting that it is fighting against the pollution caused by humans. In *Shall earth no more inspire thee*, the speaker presents nature as an actor who performs for the entertainment of humans ("Shall Nature cease to bow?"). Both examples of personification suggest a disconnected relationship between nature and humankind.

LEVELS-BASED MARK SCHEMES FOR EXTENDED RESPONSE QUESTIONS

Questions that require extended writing use levels. The whole answer will be marked together to determine which level it fits into, and which mark should be awarded within the level.

The descriptors below have been written in simple language to give an indication of the expectations of each level. See the AQA website for the official mark schemes used.

Level	Students' answers tend to include the following...
6 (26–30 marks)	• Critical, exploratory comparison supported with thoughtful and precise references. • Analysis of writer's methods with subject terminology used skilfully. Exploration of effects of writer's methods to create meanings. • Exploration of ideas / perspectives / contextual factors shown by specific, detailed links between context / text / task.
5 (21–25 marks)	• Thoughtful, developed comparison supported with apt references. • Examination of writer's methods with subject terminology used effectively. Examination of effects of writer's methods to create meanings. • Thoughtful consideration of ideas / perspectives / contextual factors shown by examination of detailed links between context / text / task.
4 (16–20 marks)	• Clear comparison supported with effective use of references. • Clear explanation of writer's methods with appropriate use of relevant subject terminology. Understanding of effects of writer's methods to create meanings. • Clear understanding of ideas / perspectives / contextual factors shown by specific links between context / text / task.
3 (11–15 marks)	• Some explained comparison. References used to support a range of relevant comments. • Explained / relevant comments on writer's methods with some relevant use of subject terminology. Identification of effects of writer's methods to create meanings. • Some understanding of implicit ideas / perspectives / contextual factors shown by links between context / text / task.
2 (6–10 marks)	• Supported comparison with some comments on references. • Identification of writer's methods, and some reference to subject terminology. • Some awareness of implicit ideas and contextual factors.
1 (1–5 marks)	• Simple comments relevant to comparison, with some reference to relevant details. • Awareness of the poet making choices, and possible reference to subject terminology. • Simple comment on ideas and contextual factors.
0 marks	Nothing worthy of credit / nothing written.

INDEX

A
A century later 25, 82
alliteration 22, 69, 110
anaphora 30, 78
Anthem for Doomed Youth 83
anthropomorphism 62
Antrobus, Raymond 100
A Portable Paradise 17, 48, 72, 106–113
assessment objectives vi
assonance 79
autobiographical 52, 107
A Wider View 41, 66–73, 80

B
ballads 12
belonging 12, 45, 53, 61, 68, 77, 92, 116
Berry, James 44
Berry, Liz 75
Black Country 76
blank verse 36
Brontë, Emily 28

C
caesura 21, 45, 86, 92, 110, 124
colonisation 52, 60
consonance 14, 79
couplets 53, 101
cyclical structure 13

D
Dharker, Imtiaz 83
dialect words 76, 79
dialogue 45
direct speech 84
dramatic monologue 29

E
Eliot, George 35
emotive language 15
end-stopping 45
England in 1819 18–25, 40, 65, 72, 120
enjambment 13, 36, 45, 53, 61, 68, 77, 84, 92, 101, 108, 124
environmental damage 36, 68, 101, 116
extended metaphor 22

F
Femi, Caleb 123
First World War 83
flashbacks 101
free verse 45, 53, 61, 68, 77, 84, 92, 101, 108, 116
French Revolution 11

G
Ghana 91
ghazal 53
Guyana 115

H
half rhymes 12
Hinduism 52
Homing 48, 57, 64, 74–81, 88
hyperbole 14

I
iambic pentameter 36
iambic tetrameter 12
iambic trimeter 12
identity 61, 77, 92, 108, 116
imperative verbs 31, 111
In a London Drawingroom 16, 32, 34–41, 121
individualism 28
Industrial Revolution 11, 35, 67
in media res 124

J
juxtaposition 14, 47, 85, 95

K
Khan, Shamshad 60
King George III 20

L
Like an Heiress 16, 81, 114–121, 128
Lines Written in Early Spring 10–17, 32, 96, 105
loneliness 29, 36, 53, 101, 108, 116
lyric poem 12

M
Maori people 100
metaphors 22, 37, 78, 79, 85, 86, 127
migration 45, 53, 61
monologues 53, 101, 108
Mundair, Raman 52
museums 60

N
Name Journeys 49, 50–57, 104, 112, 128
narrative poem 124
nature 12, 29, 36, 101, 108, 116
New Zealand 100
Nichols, Grace 115

O
On an Afternoon Train From Purley to Victoria, 1955 42–47, 64, 96, 104, 129
onomatopoeia 79, 87, 93, 102
oppression 12, 20, 84, 92, 108, 124

P
pace 92
Parker, Louisa Adjoa 91
persona poem 29
personification 14, 21, 30, 85, 118
Peterloo Massacre 19
plosive sounds 22
police discrimination 123
pot 24, 56, 58–65, 88, 97
prejudice 45, 53, 77, 124

Q
Quakers 44

R
Received Pronunciation 75
regional accents 76
repetition 31
rhetorical questions 13, 29, 31, 61, 101
Robinson, Roger 107
Romantic movement 11, 19, 28

S
Seneviratne, Seni 67
sensory language 15, 69, 93, 110
Shall earth no more inspire thee 26–33, 56, 113
Shelley, Percy Bysshe 19
sibilance 30, 54, 70, 87, 93, 102, 110
similes 38, 76, 79, 117
sonnet 20, 116
spirituality & religion 12, 29, 53

T
The Jewellery Maker 73, 90–97
Thirteen 24, 80, 89, 112, 122–129
tourism 115
Trinidad 107
triplets 22, 36, 69, 79, 119

V
volta 20, 116

W
Windrush Generation 44
With Birds You're Never Lonely 33, 40, 98–105, 120
Wordsworth, William 11

Y
Yousafzai, Malala 83

ACKNOWLEDGMENTS

The questions in this ClearRevise textbook are the sole responsibility of the authors and have neither been provided nor approved by the examination board.

Every effort has been made to trace and acknowledge ownership of copyright. The publishers will be happy to make any future amendments with copyright owners that it has not been possible to contact. The publisher would like to thank the following companies and individuals who granted permission for the use of their images in this textbook.

Image on page 11 — William Wordsworth © IanDagnall Computing / Alamy Stock Photo
Image on page 11 — The Reign of Terror © AF Fotografie / Alamy Stock Photo
Image on page 19 — Percy Bysshe Shelley © GRANGER - Historical Picture Archive / Alamy Stock Photo
Image on page 19 — Peterloo Massacre © GL Archive / Alamy Stock Photo
Image on page 28 — Emily Brontë © IanDagnall Computing / Alamy Stock Photo
Image on page 35 — George Eliot © World History Archive / Alamy Stock Photo
Image on page 35 — Victorian England skyline © Peter Righteous / Alamy Stock Photo
Image on page 44 — James Berry © Sal Idriss
Image on page 44 — Empire Windrush © World History Archive / Alamy Stock Photo
Image on page 52 — Raman Mundair with permission from Peepal Tree Press.
Image on page 52 — Rama and Sita © Art Directors & TRIP / Alamy Stock Photo
Image on page 60 — Shamshad Khan with permission from the poet
Image on page 60 — Nigerian pot © Sabena Jane Blackbird / Alamy Stock Photo
Image on page 67 — Seni Seneviratne by Sam Harwick
Image on page 67 — Marshall's Flax Mill © Chronicle / Alamy Stock Photo
Image on page 75 — Liz Berry © Thom Bartley
Image on page 75 — Family watching TV © Camerique / Alamy Stock Photo
Image on page 76 — 1925 Girl Miner Black Country © SOTK2011 / Alamy Stock Photo
Image on page 83 — Imtiaz Dharker © Ayesha Dharker Taylor
Image on page 83 — Malala Yousafzai PA Images / Alamy Stock Photo
Image on page 91 — Louisa Adjoa Parker with permission from the poet
Image on page 91 — Rural Ghana, Delali Adogla-Bessa / Shutterstock
Image on page 100 — Raymond Antrobus © SHP / Alamy Stock Photo
Image on page 100 — Maori woman, Fotos593 / Shutterstock
Image on page 107 — Roger Robinson by Naomi Woddis
Image on page 115 — Grace Nichols with permission from Bloodaxe Books
Image on page 123 — Caleb Femi © PA Images / Alamy Stock Photo
Image on page 123 — Protest in London, October 2020 Michael Tubi / Shutterstock

All other photographs and graphics ©Shutterstock

On an Afternoon Train From Purley to Victoria, 1955 by James Berry from *A Story I Am In: Selected Poems* (Bloodaxe Books, 2001).

Name Journeys by Raman Mundair, reprinted with permission from Peepal Tree Press.

Shamshad Khan *pot* from *Megalomaniac*, Salt, 2007. Commissioned by Manchester Museum 2003. By permission of Shamshad Khan. shamshadkhan.co.uk

A Wider View by Seni Seneviratne reprinted with permission from Peepal Tree Press.

Homing by Liz Berry reprinted with permission from The Random House Group.

A century later by Imtiaz Dharker from *Over the Moon* (Bloodaxe Books, 2014).

The Jewellery Maker by Louisa Adjoa Parker reprinted with permission from the poet.

With Birds You're Never Lonely © Raymond Antrobus, reproduced by kind permission by David Higham Associates.

A Portable Paradise by Roger Robinson reprinted with permission from Peepal Tree Press.

Like an Heiress by Grace Nichols from *I Have Crossed an Ocean: Selected Poems* (Bloodaxe Books, 2010).

Thirteen by Caleb Femi from *Poor*. Reprinted with permission from Penguin Books Ltd.

EXAMINATION TIPS

With your examination practice, use a boundary approximation using the following table. Be aware that the grade boundaries can vary from year to year, so they should be used as a guide only.

Grade	9	8	7	6	5	4	3	2	1
Boundary	88%	79%	71%	61%	52%	43%	31%	21%	10%

1. Read the question carefully. Don't give an answer to a question that you *think* is appearing (or wish was appearing!) rather than the actual question.
2. It's worth jotting down a quick plan to make sure your answer includes sufficient detail and is focused on the question.
3. Start your answer with a brief introduction where you summarise the main points of your response. This can help your answer to stay on-track.
4. Your answer can include the poets' language choices, but also structural choices (such as the ordering of stanzas), themes, and tone.
5. Include details from the poems to support your answer. These details might be quotes, or they can be references to the poems.
6. Examiners tend to award more marks to answers that focus on a smaller number of details in more depth, than a wider variety of points in limited detail. So don't feel pressured to comment on everything in the poems, in fact, concentrating on a few key points can often be more worthwhile.
7. Make sure your handwriting is legible. The examiner can't award you marks if they are unable to read what you've written.
8. The examiner will be impressed if you can correctly use technical terms like 'quatrains', 'metaphor', 'allegory', 'personification' etc, but to get the best marks you need to explore the effect of these techniques on the reader.
9. Use linking words and phrases to show you are developing your points or comparing information, for example, "this reinforces", "this shows that" and "on the other hand". This helps to give your answer structure, and makes it easier for the examiner to award you marks.
10. If you need extra paper, make sure you clearly signal that your answer is continued elsewhere. Remember that longer answers don't necessarily score more highly than shorter, more concise answers.

Good luck!

New titles **coming soon!**

Revision, re-imagined

These guides are everything you need to ace your exams and beam with pride. Each topic is laid out in a beautifully illustrated format that is clear, approachable and as concise and simple as possible.

They have been expertly compiled and edited by subject specialists, highly experienced examiners, industry professionals and a good dollop of scientific research into what makes revision most effective. Past examination questions are essential to good preparation, improving understanding and confidence.

- Hundreds of marks worth of examination style questions
- Answers provided for all questions within the books
- Illustrated topics to improve memory and recall
- Specification references for every topic
- Examination tips and techniques
- Free Python solutions pack (CS Only)

Absolute clarity is the aim.

Explore the series and add to your collection at **www.clearrevise.com**

Available from all good book shops

  @pgonlinepub

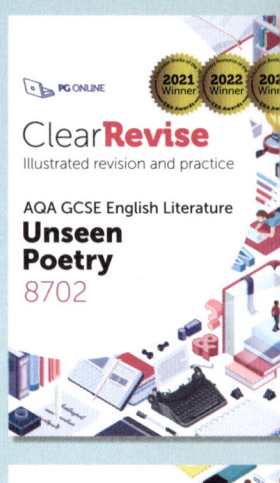

ClearRevise
Illustrated revision and practice
AQA GCSE English Literature
Unseen Poetry
8702

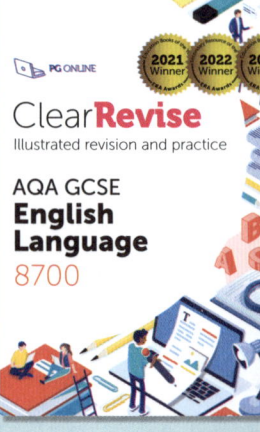

ClearRevise
Illustrated revision and practice
AQA GCSE
English Language
8700

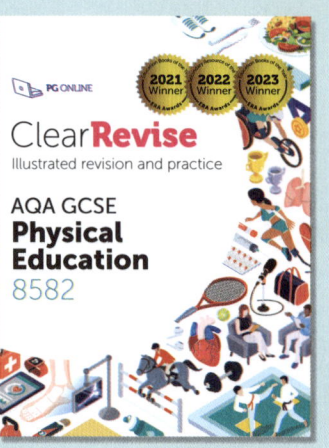

ClearRevise
Illustrated revision and practice
AQA GCSE
Physical Education
8582

ClearRevise
Illustrated revision and practice
Edexcel GCSE
History 1HI0
Weimar and Nazi Germany, 1918–39
Paper 3

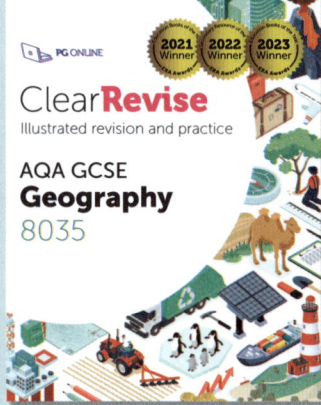

ClearRevise
Illustrated revision and practice
AQA GCSE
Geography
8035

ClearRevise
Illustrated revision and practice
OCR GCSE
Computer Science
J277

ClearRevise
Illustrated revision and practice
AQA GCSE English Literature
Macbeth
By William Shakespeare
8702

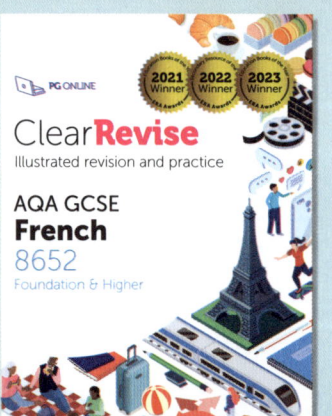

ClearRevise
Illustrated revision and practice
AQA GCSE
French
8652
Foundation & Higher

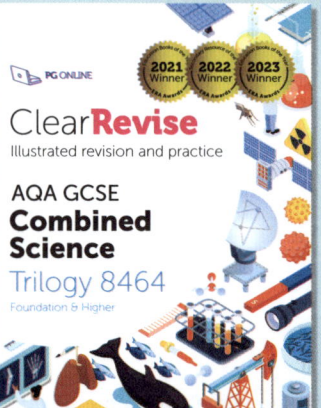

ClearRevise
Illustrated revision and practice
AQA GCSE
Combined Science
Trilogy 8464
Foundation & Higher

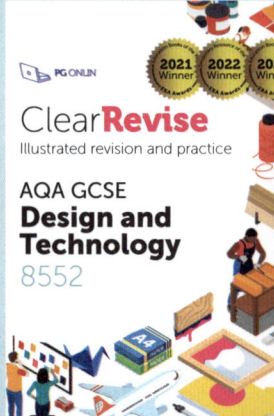

ClearRevise
Illustrated revision and practice
AQA GCSE
Design and Technology
8552